Prisonization, Friendship, and Leadership

Prisonization, Friendship, and Leadership

John A. Slosar, Jr.
St. Louis University

Lexington Books
D.C. Heath and Company
Lexington, Massachusetts
Toronto

45329

Library of Congress Cataloging in Publication Data

Slosar, John A.
    Prisonization, friendship, and leadership.

    Bibliography: p.
    1. Prison psychology. 2. Friendship. 3. Leadership. 4. Juvenile correc-
tions. I. Title.
HV6089.S57   365'.6   77-14698
ISBN 0-669-02023-0

Copyright © 1978 by D.C. Heath and Company

All rights reserved. No part of this publication may be reproduced or transmit-
ted in any form or by any means, electronic or mechanical, including
photocopy, recording, or any information storage or retrieval system, without
permission in writing from the publisher.

Published simultaneously in Canada

Printed in the United States of America

International Standard Book Number: 0-669-02023-0

Library of Congress Catalog Card Number: 77-14698

*To Betsy, as always
and forever.*

Contents

45329

List of Tables

Acknowledgments

The debt of gratitude owed by any author is a great one. This instance is far from being an exception to that rule.

The research on which this book was based was conducted as part of a larger comparative study of correctional programs for youthful offenders funded by the Bureau of Prisons, U.S. Department of Justice. Codirectors of the larger research project were Robert Vinter and Rosemary Sarri of The University of Michigan. The points of view and opinions stated in this book are the sole responsibility of the author and do not necessarily represent the positions of the project directors or the Bureau of Prisons.

Special appreciation is expressed to Norman Carlson, Director of the Bureau of Prisons, and to H.G. Moeller, Howard Kitchener, John Conrad, and Roy Gerard of the Bureau of Prisons at the time of the research and to all the staff and young men at Federal East and Federal West without whose cooperation this book would not have been possible.

I am also indebted to Henry Meyer, Rosemary Sarri, Martin Gold, Colin Loftin, and John Tropman, all of whom read and commented on earlier drafts of the book. Rosemary Sarri, through her encouragement and example, was especially instrumental in bringing this work to fruition.

Many friends and colleagues, both in Ann Arbor and in St. Louis, assisted me through their consultation and encouragement. I would also like to thank Gloria Quade and Laura Richmond for their painstaking efforts in typing earlier versions of the manuscript.

Last, but certainly not least, I must acknowledge the contributions of my wife Betsy, who not only provided the support and encouragement without which I could not have survived much less have persisted in this undertaking, but who also contributed directly to this work by typing the first draft, applying first aid to my many grammatical fractures, and proofreading many pages many times.

For the deficiencies of this book, whether of fact or inference, the author alone assumes responsibility.

Prisonization, Friendship, and Leadership

1 Some Musing on a Grim Tale: The Alternate Society

Once upon a time, 1940 to be exact, a sociologist wrote of a strange community to which men were temporarily banished because they were possessed by evil spirits. Although high priests were sent to visit the banished men, their efforts to drive out the evil spirits proved in vain. The banished men resisted the efforts of the high priests and withdrew from them, speaking a strange language and living by rules foreign to the high priests. Under these conditions the evil spirits in many of the men, instead of withering away, increased and multiplied. Thus, when the men were finally allowed to return to the land from which they came, the people found them possessed by spirits more numerous and more evil than before, and they caused the men to be banished again and again.

Clemmer originally used the term *prisonization* to indicate "the taking on in greater or less degree of the folkways, mores, customs, and general culture of the penitentiary." Foremost among the elements of the prison culture which the prisonized inmate embraced was the inmate code, which prohibited cooperation with staff and demanded unqualified loyalty among inmates, especially in opposition to the prison staff. He hypothesized that, while the prisonization process might be irregular, in general, the longer the inmate was in prison, the more prisonized he was likely to become.[1]

It has been almost forty years since Clemmer postulated his prisonization hypothesis in his classic work *The Prison Community*, but social scientists and prison administrators are still not certain how much of it should be classified as a grim tale and how much of it should be treated as grim reality.

To what extent does prisonization occur? Is prisonization merely the manifestation of behavior and attitudes that offenders bring with them into the correctional institution, or is it a reaction to the pains of imprisonment? What kinds of social relationships characterize the inmate society? Who becomes a leader? Who becomes a follower? Who become friends? What is the impact of segregating criminal offenders from the rest of society and requiring that they live in settings peopled primarily by other criminal offenders?

These are serious questions, questions that have important implications. They are especially relevant given the intensifying debate regarding the efficacy of correctional rehabilitation efforts, the demands for a moratorium on the construction of prisons, efforts to close state institutions for delinquent youth, and the attempts to remove juvenile status offenders from the justice system. The answers to these questions are of importance not only

1

to the social scientist and prison administrator, but also to policymakers, legislators, and citizens as taxpayers. Lest we forget, we also ought to mention the import of these answers for those whom society classifies as criminal offenders.

The purpose of this book is to approach these questions by examining patterns of prisonization, integration, leadership, and friendship found in two federal youth centers, which we shall call Federal East and Federal West. Before going on to describe Federal East and Federal West in detail and presenting our findings, we first will review some of the previous work done in this area and present the conceptual framework which guided this analysis.

Previous Models of the Inmate Group

The distinctive social roles and relationships, norms, argot, and various cultural elements that are characteristic of inmate groups have at various times been labeled the "culture of the prison,"[2] the "society of captives,"[3] or more recently, the "inmate contraculture."[4] There have been numerous attempts to explain the emergence of the inmate social system and the congruence or conflict between its normative content and that of the officially imposed norms and values of the institution. Cline has grouped these various explanations under two general models: the *direct importation* and the *deprivation* models of prisonization. In the direct importation model, the extent to which the inmate society promotes values in opposition to the staff depends on the inmates' experience and commitment to criminal value systems prior to their incarceration. The inmates "import" or bring into the institution the same values they held outside the institution. The antisocial values they held while free take the form of opposition to the official authorities of the institution.[5] Irwin and Cressey are among the most explicit proponents of this interpretation. They argue that the "prison code" prohibiting cooperation with staff is part of a larger, more general criminal code that exists outside of the prison. The inmates bring with them into the prison setting a variety of cultural patterns, some of them products of previous institutional experience. Consequently, it is not possible to understand inmate behavior by looking at a "prison culture" that is seen solely or even primarily as a reaction to the conditions of incarceration.[6]

Cline, in a study of fifteen Scandinavian prisons, found strong support for the importation model.[7] Thomas and Foster have argued that the inmates' expectations of their life chances after release from prison have an important impact on the degree and direction of the prisonization process.[8]

In the deprivation model of prisonization the extent to which the inmate society promotes values in opposition to the staff depends on the degree of physical, psychological, and social deprivation and degradation imposed on the inmates by the institutional setting. The inmate subsystem is seen as a collective response to the pains of imprisonment. Sykes has discussed in detail the various deprivations the inmates must cope with: the deprivation of liberty, the deprivation of goods and services, the deprivation of heterosexual relationships, the deprivation of autonomy, the deprivation of security, and the deprivation of self-esteem. One of the only ways the inmates have of dealing with these deprivations is by creating a society of their own within which scarce resources may be reallocated, social identities maintained, and one's self-esteem salvaged.

Unable to escape either physically or psychologically, lacking the cohesion to carry through an insurrection that is bound to fail in any case, and bereft of faith in peaceful innovation, the inmate population might seem to have no recourse but the simple endurance of the pains of imprisonment. The frustrations and deprivations of confinement, with their attendant attacks on the prisoner's self-image, would strike the prisoner with full force and the time spent in prison would have to be marked down as time spent in purgatory. And to a large extent this is what does happen in reality. There are no exits for the inmate in the sense of a device or series of devices which can completely eliminate the pains of imprisonment. *But if the rigors of confinement cannot be completely removed, they can at least be mitigated by the patterns of social interaction established among the inmates themselves.* In this apparently simple fact lies the key to our understanding of the prisoner's world.[9]

Thus, the inmate society is seen as a reaction to deprivations imposed by the correctional institution. Street, in a comparative study of inmate groups in juvenile correctional institutions, took a similar view of the inmate subculture, linking it directly to the larger organizational context in which it is located.

As we see it, such social and political dimensions of the inmate system can best be linked to the patterns of the larger organization when they are organized around a conception of the inmate system as an adaptive, problem-solving group. In this view, the group is analyzed as reactive to the major features of its environment. Thus, the crucial link between the organization and the inmate system is seen to be the nature of the problems which the institutional environment presents to the inmates (primarily through the balance of gratifications and deprivations) and the nature of the context within which it determines that these problems must be solved (primarily through the patterns of authority and control).[10]

Those researchers who have been characterized as working under the importation model tend to emphasize the open-system characteristics of the prison; those utilizing a deprivation model tend to emphasize the closed-system characteristics. While neither school of thought has completely ignored the variables deemed important by the other, it is only rather recently that emphasis has been placed on determining what importance should be assigned to each. The theoretical and empirical evidence in support of the deprivation model is substantial, but much of the data are also congruent with the importation model, and there is a need to determine the relative utility of each. The conclusions of Irwin and Cressey, Cline, and Thomas and Foster, which stress the importance of the importation model, already have been cited. Recently, yet another group of researchers has called for additional attention to be given to the importation model in conceptualizing the inmate group. After a rather intensive study of the inmate population of a treatment-oriented, medium security institution in California, Kassebaum, Ward, and Wilner concluded that the "old model" of the prison as a closed social system in which severe deprivations result in an inmate code (through which the inmates cope with these deprivations) is no longer appropriate. Rather, they argue that

1. Many prisons are not self-contained and isolated systems but are relatively permeable units in larger systems called departments of corrections.

2. Because of differences in the conditions of imprisonment between departments of corrections and between prisons of higher or lower security ratings within the same department, inmates in prisons throughout the United States are reacting to very different combinations of material, social, and psychological deprivations.

3. The preprison backgrounds of inmates influence the kinds of adaptations that are made to combat the pains of imprisonment.[11]

Thus, there is evidence supporting both the importation and the deprivation models of prisonization. There is a growing awareness of the need to combine the two in a balanced perspective to understand more fully the informal organization of the inmate group. It is this issue that we will now address.

A Proposed Model: The Alternate Society

We would like to propose that the informal adaptations of the inmate group may be fruitfully conceptualized as an "alternate society," that is, an alternate social structure through which the inmate occupants seek to meet their physical, psychological, and social needs. It is a means by which the inmates attempt to obtain those gratifications denied them by the institution by virtue of their status as inmates. Inmate group formation with the accompanying group norms, communication channels, and association structures will take place in all institutional settings. The degree to which informal networks are developed and elaborated and the extent to which the normative content of those structures will be congruent with staff norms and values will, however, vary from institution to institution. We will focus on the factors that appear to be most directly related to these two aspects of the alternate society, the degree of elaboration, and the degree of congruency with the staff-endorsed normative system. We should, however, at this point emphasize that we do not see the informal inmate system or what we have termed the alternate society, per se, as being either desirable or undesirable, but rather as an inevitable fact of social life. Within any formal organization one can locate patterns of social regularities that sociologists have labeled informal organization. However, such systems of informal organization do vary in the extent to which they successfully meet the needs of their members and the impact they have on the attainment of the goals of the formal organization. While much attention in the literature has been given to the negative aspects of the inmate system, this form of informal organization may also be seen as serving a number of positive functions, both in meeting the real and pressing needs of the inmates and in supporting institutional change efforts. In other words, the inmate system may be positive or negative in its impact on the achievement of inmate and organizational goals, and we may learn as much, if not more, about the inmate system by studying these positive functions and their determinants as we would if we focused solely on the negative aspects.

While this formulation of the alternate society emphasizes the inmate system as a collective problemsolving mechanism, it does not necessitate a choice between the deprivation and importation models of the inmate system. Rather it provides a more general theoretical perspective in which these two models may be linked, providing guidelines as to when emphasis on one rather than the other of these models may be more fruitful. In viewing the inmate group as an alternate society we are emphasizing the importance of both the informal social structure and the characteristics of the occupants of that structure. Both categories of variables and their possible interaction must be considered if we are to fully understand the alternate society.

The deprivation model of prisonization stresses the closed-system aspects of the prison experience; the informal inmate system is an attempt to overcome the pains of imprisonment and avoid self-rejection by rejecting the rejectors. In this model the constraints and deprivations imposed by the institution and institutional staff are seen as the major independent variables that affect the nature of the inmate system. The importation model of prisonization, while acknowledging the influence of the deprivations and pressures of imprisonment, emphasizes the open-system aspects of the correctional institution—factors external to the immediate situation in which the inmates find themselves. The normative content of the inmate system is not seen as a logical outcome of the problems of imprisonment but rather as having its roots in the preprison experiences of inmates in the criminal subculture.

The concept of the alternate society is based on the basic notion that the official social structure of the correctional institution fails through oversight, design, or limited resources to meet the basic needs of the inmates. There is a discrepancy between what is sought and what is provided. At first glance this appears to be little more than a straightforward restatement of the deprivation model of prisonization, but the emphasis here is on the *discrepancy* or *difference* between what the inmates seek and what the institution provides or allows. This difference may come about in a number of ways. The institution may place severe constraints and deprivations on the inmate, denying him what would otherwise be available and legitimate gratifications in the outside world. Such restrictions may force even relatively prosocial inmates into taking stances contrary to the staff-imposed normative structure in order to meet their basic physical, psychological, and social needs. On the other hand, the institution may provide a relatively liberal gratification-deprivation balance, but the inmates may bring with them demands or life-styles that are in conflict with or go beyond even the liberal provisions of the institution. In this case a discrepancy again exists. In sum, a discrepancy that produces conditions conducive to the existence of a negatively oriented inmate society may be a result of extreme variations in the demands brought to the situation by either the correctional setting or the inmate population. The extreme situation is found where we have not only antisocial inmates who would find even an institution with a relatively permissive normative structure and favorable gratification-deprivation balance unsatisfactory, but also an organizational setting characterized by a restrictive normative structure and a relatively unfavorable gratification-deprivation balance. It is here that we are most likely to find the most negative orientations of the inmates toward the institution and staff and the negative aspects of the alternate society in their most developed forms. Conversely, where we find the intersection of a relatively prosocial inmate population and an organizational setting characterized by a relatively permissive normative structure and a favorable gratification-deprivation balance, we are least likely to encounter negative group adaptations. It is in this set of circumstances that various aspects of the inmate alternate society are likely to be congruent with and supportive of the staff's normative structure and rehabilitative change goals. It is also under this set of circumstances that we would expect to find the more desirable—from a humanistic perspective—forms of interpersonal relationships, relationships that could be characterized as primary and expressive rather than the instrumental or parasitical relations that are likely to exist under the other set of extreme circumstances. There are two possible intermediate situations: (1) where we have antisocial inmates and a permissive normative structure with a favorable gratification-deprivation balance, and (2) where we have prosocial inmates and a restrictive normative structure with an unfavorable gratification-deprivation balance.

In the former situation organizational conditions are likely to promote prostaff and proinstitutional adaptations and have a counteracting effect on the probability of antistaff and anti-institutional adaptations coming about. The basis for opposing staff will be minimal, and a condition of scarce resources (necessary for the power base of negatively oriented inmate leaders) will also be lacking. In the latter situation organizational conditions may very well induce antistaff and anti-institutional adaptations on the part of the inmates, even though these may have been contrary to the initial predispositions of prosocial inmates. A restrictive organizational climate may force relatively prosocial inmates to utilize informal adaptations in violation of staff norms in order to meet what they see as basic and legitimate needs. Involvement in such informal adaptations may lead to entanglement in a system of norms and obligations encompassing areas far removed from the basic needs the inmate originally sought to satisfy. For this reason we would argue that custodially and punitively oriented institutions with relatively restrictive organizational climates are more likely to provide the circumstances eliciting negative adaptations among the inmates than other institutions that provide a more permissive organizational climate.

We have attempted to predict how two major categories of variables derived from the deprivation and importation models of prisonization will affect the character of the adaptations arrived at by the inmate groups. However, the orientations of the inmates and character of the organizational climates are continuous rather than discrete, dichotomous variables; likewise there are more than four values possible for the variable of inmate adaptations. When we speak of nonprisonized and prisonized responses to the incarceration experience we are not referring to discrete categories of responses to the prison situation but rather to the extremes of a continuum of responses. Prisonization is not a "yes" or "no" matter but rather a question of degree.

In sum, this then is the theoretical model, the alternate society, which will guide our analysis and for which we shall seek confirmation or disconfirmation:

The informal social adaptations of the inmates constitute an alternate society, that is, an alternate social structure through which the inmate occupants seek to meet their physical, psychological and social needs. The character of this "society" will be significantly influenced by (1) the type of organizational climate which prevails in the institution, and (2) the predispositions which the inmates bring with them to the situation.

We believe that this model allows us greater understanding of previous research findings and will prove to be a more fruitful starting point for future research.

Notes

1. Donald Clemmer, *The Prison Community* (New York: Holt, Rinehart and Winston, 1958) pp. 299, 152.

2. Ibid., pp. 85-86.

3. Gresham M. Sykes, *The Society of Captives; A Study of a Maximum Security Prison* (New York: Atheneum, 1966).

4. Charles W. Thomas, "Toward a More Inclusive Model of the Inmate Contraculture," *Criminology* 8 (1970): 251-262.

5. Hugh F. Cline, "The Determinants of Normative Patterns in Correctional Institutions," in *Scandinavian Studies in Criminology*, ed. Nils Christie, (Oslo: Oslo University Press, 1968) vol. 2., pp. 173-184.

6. John Irwin and Donald R. Cressey, "Thieves, Convicts and the Inmate Culture," *Social Problems* 10 (1962): 142-155.

7. Cline, "Determinants of Normative Patterns."

8. Charles W. Thomas and Samuel C. Foster, "Prisonization in the Inmate Contraculture," *Social Problems* 20 (1972): 229-239.

9. Sykes, *Society of Captives*, p. 82.

10. David Street, "The Inmate Social Organization: A Comparative Study of Juvenile Correctional Institutions" (Ph.D. dissertation, University of Michigan, 1962), pp. 44-45.

11. Gene Kassebaum, David Ward, and Daniel Wilner, *Prison Treatment and Parole Survival: An Empirical Assessment* (New York: John Wiley and Sons, 1971), p. 298.

2

Hypotheses Regarding
the Alternate Society

In this chapter we will elaborate on the model of the alternate society as we explicate a series of hypotheses dealing with prisonization, integration, friendship patterns, and leadership patterns among inmates. These hypotheses have been derived from, or at the very least are congruent with, our conception of the alternate society and previous research in this area.

Major Variables Affecting the Alternate Society

The nature of the alternate society will be significantly influenced by the following factors:

Hypothesis 1a *Inmate groups in permissive organizational climates will be characterized by nonprisonized adaptations; inmate groups in restrictive organizational climates will be characterized by prisonized adaptations.*

Hypothesis 1b *Inmates with relatively prosocial backgrounds will manifest nonprisonized adaptations to the institutional experience; inmates with relatively antisocial backgrounds will manifest prisonized adaptations to the institutional experience.*

Hypothesis 1c *The organizational climate of the institution and the preinstitutional orientations of the inmates will interact with additive effects resulting in extreme nonprisonized or prisonized adaptations or with cancelling effects resulting in adaptations of an intermediate variety.*

Hypothesis 1d *The organizational climate within which the inmates are located will be of primary importance in influencing the adaptation of the inmates; the preinstitutional orientations of the inmates constitute an important, although secondary, influence on the adaptations of the inmates.*

Prisonized adaptations are those that are in accord with the so-called inmate code and that violate the staff's definition of appropriate behavior. Permissive and restrictive organizational climates refer to the overall balance of freedom and gratifications and deprivations that characterizes the organizational setting in which the inmates are found. Prosocial and antisocial backgrounds refer to the socialization experiences of the inmate prior to this institutional commitment.

9

Hypotheses 1a and 1b are restatements of the basic propositions that underlie the deprivation and importation models of the inmate group, of which the alternate society is a composite. Hypothesis 1a, a restatement of the deprivation model, states that in permissive organizational climates inmates will not manifest prisonized adaptations. Hypothesis 1b is a restatement of the importation model of the inmate system; inmates with preinstitutional prosocial orientations are also less likely to utilize prisonized adaptations. Hypotheses 1a and 1b state that both deprivation model variables and importation model variables are related to the nature of the alternate society of inmates. In Hypotheses 1c and 1d we attempt to specify the relationships that exist between these two classes of variables. Hypothesis 1c predicts that the organizational climate and preinstitutional orientations may interact, resulting in either extreme instances of non-prisonized adaptations, very prisonized adaptations, or intermediate forms of adjustment. We would expect to approximate the first of these conditions where we find a permissive organizational climate and prosocial inmates; we would expect to approximate the second of these conditions where we have a very restrictive organizational climate and antisocial inmates; we would expect to find intermediate forms of adaptations where we have intermediate values of these independent variables or where we have combinations resulting in mixed circumstances, e.g., a permissive organizational climate and antisocial inmates. Hypothesis 1d predicts that the deprivation variables will be more powerful than the importation variables in terms of predicting the adaptations of the inmate group. We have proposed previously that a permissive organizational climate would tend to deter the emergence of negative adaptations, since the basis for opposing staff will be minimal, and a condition of scarce resources—an important ingredient of the power base of negatively oriented inmate leaders—will be also lacking. Conversely, a restrictive organizational climate may force even relatively prosocial inmates into utilizing antistaff and anti-institutional adaptations to satisfy what they consider legitimate needs.

Integration within the Alternate Society

One of the more basic questions that can be asked about the inmate society is the extent to which inmates participate in it. How often do inmates spend their free time in the company of other inmates? How many friendships have they established with other inmates? How much do they value these friendships? In short, how integrated or how much a part of an inmate group are the individual inmates? We believe that integration within the alternate society of inmates will vary with the organizational climate and background characteristics of the inmates in the following ways:

Hypothesis 2a *Inmates located in institutions characterized by permissive organizational climates will have more highly developed patterns of integration and primary relations than will inmates in institutions characterized by restrictive organizational climates.*

Hypothesis 2b *Voluntary interaction among inmates will vary directly with the amount of interaction between staff and inmates.*

Hypothesis 2c *Integration is related to the phase of the inmate's institutional career, being low at the beginning of confinement, increasing toward the middle, and decreasing toward release.*

Hypothesis 2d *Integration of the inmate group will vary inversely with the heterogeneity of the inmate group.*

Hypothesis 2e *Integration among inmates is inversely related to the amount of correctional confinement they have experienced.*

Hypothesis 2f *Integration among inmates is inversely related to the age of the inmates.*

Hypothesis 2g *Integration among the inmates is inversely related to the intensity and extensiveness of extrainstitutional ties maintained by the inmates.*

Hypotheses 2a, 2b, 2c, and 2d emphasize the closed-system aspects of the incarceration experience. Integration among inmates is seen as varying with the overall organizational climate, the amount of contact inmates have with staff, and the phase of their own institutional career.

Hypothesis 2a states that inmates in permissive organizational climates will have more highly developed patterns of integration and primary relations than will inmates in restrictive organizational climates. We expect this to be the case for a number of reasons. First, the greater freedom of movement and lack of constraints to be found in permissive organizational settings will serve to facilitate rather than hinder associations. We would expect the reverse to be true in restrictive organizational climates. Secondly, the more favorable balance of gratification and deprivation to be found in the permissive organizational climate will also facilitate a wide range of associations established for expressive rather than competitive instrumental purposes. Consequently, we have hypothesized that the patterns of integration and primary relations will be more highly developed in institutions with permissive organizational climates.

Many of the factors which underlie the establishment and maintenance of permissive organizational climates, e.g., treatment goals and benign perceptions of inmates, are likely to result also in the willingness of staff to interact on an informal basis with the inmates. Further, under such conditions staff are less likely to view interaction among the inmates as inappropriate or threatening. On the contrary, they may even encourage extensive interaction among the inmates. As a result, we have predicted in Hypothesis 2b that voluntary interaction among inmates will be directly correlated with the amount of interaction that takes place between staff and inmates.

Hypothesis 2c posits a curvilinear relationship between integration and the phase of the inmate's institutional career. At the beginning of the inmate's incarceration he will still be oriented toward the outside world and may possibly still have very strong ties to other persons outside the institution. The longer the inmate is in the institution, the greater the time distance between him and his outside interests and the more tenuous his ties to persons outside the institution are likely to become. More of his life becomes focused on events and persons within the institution, and he becomes involved in friendships within the inmate group. At the middle phase of his institutional career he is timewise most distant from life outside the institution and most involved in the life of the institution. However, as he approaches release, this process reverses itself. The inmate begins to reorient himself to life outside the institution in anticipation of his release and becomes less involved in social relationships within the institution. The relationship predicted here was originally reported by Wheeler and was later supported by the findings of Garabedian and Glaser.[1] A more recent attempt by Atchley and McCabe to replicate Wheeler's findings did not find the inverted U-shaped relationship between career phase and integration; but they did find that integration regularly increased as the inmates moved through the early to middle to late phases of their institutional careers.[2] This failure to replicate the earlier findings of Wheeler and others introduces the possibility that the relationship between career phase and integration may vary from institution to institution and that other variables may be involved. Presently we do not have enough information to predict a relationship other than that stated above.

In Hypothesis 2d we have predicted that the overall degree of integration of the inmate group will vary inversely with the heterogeneity of the inmate group. People tend to enter into personal relationships with others who are similar to themselves. The greater the heterogeneity of the inmate group, the fewer the opportunities to associate with others similar to one's self.

Hypotheses 2e and 2f involve variables that could be classified as importation variables and that emphasize the open-system nature of the alternate society. Hypothesis 2e states that integration among inmates is inversely related to the amount of previous institutionalization they have experienced. The argument here is that the more experiences they have had in institutions, the more likely they are to have learned to "pull their own time" and "stick to themselves." Hypothesis 2f states that integration will be inversely related to age. Young inmates will spend more time with a larger number of other inmates than will older inmates. In this respect younger inmates may resemble their noninstitutionalized counterparts in having many friends or acquaintances. Older inmates will be more discriminate in maintaining a few relationships on which they can rely more heavily. In sum, the institution-wise and mature inmates are more likely to have few friends and a more constricted set of relationships in the institution in contrast to the institution-naive and younger inmates who attempt a wide range of relationships similar to those they knew on the outside.

Hypothesis 2g in stating that integration is inversely related to extrainstitutional contacts also focuses on the open-system aspects of the correctional institution. To the extent that the inmate is able to maintain or even establish extrainstitutional ties during the period of his incarceration, he will have less need of friends within the institution to provide for various social and psychological needs. The inmate who has no contacts with others outside the institution will of necessity turn to his fellow inmates.

Integration and Inmate Adaptations

Integration will be related to inmate orientations in the following manner:

Hypothesis 3a *Integration in the inmate group in institutions characterized by permissive organizational climates will be related to nonprisonized orientations on the part of the inmates.*

Hypothesis 3b *Integration in the inmate group in institutions characterized by restrictive organizational climates will be related to prisonized orientations on the part of the inmates.*

Hypothesis 3c *The accuracy of the inmates' perceptions of the orientations of the other inmates will be related to integration within the inmate group.*

In keeping with our earlier formulation, we predict that inmate group formation in institutions characterized by permissive organizational climates is more likely to be tolerated if not actually encouraged by the staff and is likely to be based on factors other than opposition to the staff. The balance of gratifications and deprivations in such settings will make it more profitable for the inmates to cooperate with rather than oppose staff. Further, the functions served by the inmate group in such settings are more likely to be of a socioemotional or expressive rather than instrumental nature. Under such circumstances the general impact of the inmate group will be a positive one, and inmates who are integrated into the inmate group will be a more positive and less prisonized than those who are unintegrated. This was the finding of Street, Vinter, and Perrow in their study of six juvenile correctional institutions.[3] Conversely, in those settings characterized by restrictive organizational climates, integration into the inmate group will be related to negative orientations toward the staff and institution and more prisonized responses by the inmates. In such settings inmate group formation is less likely to receive the approval of the staff; the balance of gratifications and deprivations is more likely to be such as to elicit illegitimate adaptations by the inmates in obtaining and reallocating scarce resources. The inmate group in these circumstances is more likely to be instrumentally rather than expressively oriented.

A number of correctional researchers have reported the phenomenon of "pluralistic ignorance"—a marked tendency for inmates to perceive erroneously other inmates as having less commitment to staff-supported values than is, in fact, the case.[4] Such perceptions or misperceptions are related to the quantity and quality of communication, which itself is a function of the integration of the inmate in the inmate group. The more integrated the inmate within the inmate group and the greater the quantity and more open the quality of the communications he shares with others, the more accurate will be his perceptions of the values and norms endorsed by the other inmates. Further findings regarding the factors that affect the condition of "pluralistic ignorance" could be of import for creating conditions conducive to rehabilitative change. If inmates actually do believe others are more negatively oriented than they really are, then perhaps more open communication and a more open sharing of one's private commitments may dramatically alter the normative climate of the alternate society of inmates.

Friendships within the Alternate Society

On the basis of our model of the informal inmate system as an alternate society and previous theoretical work in this area, we predict that the friendship choices of the inmates will be affected by the following variables:

Hypothesis 4a *Friendship choices among the inmates will vary with propinquity or physical proximity.*

Hypothesis 4b *Inmates will tend to choose as friends other inmates who are similar to themselves in terms of various personal, offense, and organizational characteristics.*

Hypothesis 4c *The friendship choices of inmates in restrictive organizational climates will show a greater tendency to be structured along personal, offense, and organizational categories than the friendship choices of in-mates in permissive organizational climates.*

Hypothesis 4d *Inmates will tend to be similar to the inmates they choose as friends in terms of their normative orientations.*

The closer two people are to each other, the greater the potential for their interaction; the more often they interact, the more likely they are to like each other. There is a substantial amount of evidence reported in the literature on interpersonal attraction that documents this important role of propinquity or physical proximity. We would expect, then, that inmates who live together in the same housing units and participate together in organizational program activities will be more likely to choose each other as friends. Since even the most open institution will still find it necessary to limit the movement of the inmates, we may expect this variable to be of even greater significance in the institutional setting than it is in other settings.

Although they do not agree as to exactly why, most social psychologists do agree that similarity in terms of various demographic and psychological variables is related to interpersonal attraction. Similarity in terms of socioeconomic status, religion, sex, age, intelligence, ability, and self-description apparently leads to interpersonal attraction. Where we have a range of educational and urban-rural backgrounds represented within an in-stitutional population we would expect these variables also to have some im-pact on the inmates' choices of friends. Although there is little in the way of statistical data on which we may build, the observations and theoretical for-mulations of Irwin would lead us to believe that friendship choices of in-mates will also be influenced by the criminal identities of the inmates themselves: Thieves will associate with thieves, drug users with drug users, etc.[5] Therefore we will be examining offense histories as possible indicators of the inmates' criminal identities and looking to see if a relationship does exist between this indicator and the inmate's choice of friends.

Most of the variables discussed above were found to be related to in-terpersonal attraction in settings other than, and often quite different from, the correctional institution. Our consideration of these variables will be focused on determining which variables are the most important in terms of structuring friendships in the correctional institution. It is likely that some variables that were found to be related to friendship choices in more open settings will be of lesser significance. The importance of various characteristics may vary not only from noninstitutional to institutional set-tings, but also from institution to institution. Hypothesis 4c predicts one such type of variation: Personal, offense, and organizationally assigned categories will be of greater significance in structuring friendship choices in restrictive organizational climates than in permissive organizational climates. What we have termed a permissive organizational climate—an organizational climate characterized by a relatively favorable balance of gratifications and deprivations and a relatively liberal normative structure—will have an impact not only on the relations between inmates and staff but also on the relations among the inmates themselves. Interpersonal relationships in permissive settings will tend to be more open and based on the ability of the inmates to meet each other's socioemotional needs; interpersonal relationships in restrictive organizational settings will tend to be of a more utilitarian and exploitative nature. In the latter situation inmates may have neither the opportunity nor the willingness to become acquainted and familiar with a wide range of others in the institution, and associations will tend to be based on external and readily discernible criteria such as similarity of age, race, and offense. In the permissive setting conditions are such as to encourage the cutting across of such boundaries to a much greater extent, and friendships will not as often be limited by external formal criteria.

Hypothesis 4d posits a relationship between friendship choice and similarity of normative orientations. Although some debate remains regarding the theoretical explanation of the relationship, the relationship between attraction and congruity of attitudes, beliefs, and values is one of the best-documented in the literature. We have no reason to believe that this should be any different within correctional institutions, and we would expect that the inmates would choose as friends other inmates whose normative orientations toward the staff and institution were similar to their own.

Leadership Patterns within the Alternate Society

A review of the social psychological literature leads one to the conclusion that the personality and background characteristics that distinguish leaders from nonleaders are contingent on the demands of the situation:

A person does not become a leader by virtue of his possession of any one particular pattern of personality traits, but the pattern of personal characteristics of the leader must bear relevant relationship to the present characteristics, activities, and goals of the group of which he is leader.[6]

All correctional institutions share certain basic characteristics and differ in others. The problems they present to the inmates are similar in some respects but different in others. We would predict, therefore, that the inmate leaders in these institutions will be similar in some respects but different in others. Previous research indicates that there are certain characteristics that we can expect to be associated with leadership status under various conditions.

We predict that leaderships status in the alternate society of inmates will be related to the following personal, offense, and organizationally assigned characteristics:

Hypothesis 5a *Leadership status will be related to length of stay in the institution. Leaders will have been in the institution longer than nonleaders.*

Hypothesis 5b *Age will be related to leadership status in juvenile and youth institutions: Leaders in general will be older than nonleaders.*

Hypothesis 5c *In general, inmate leaders will have more education than nonleaders.*

Hypothesis 5d *Inmate leaders will have more serious offense histories in terms of the types and numbers of offenses than will nonleaders.*

Hypothesis 5e *Relatively uncooperative and negative leaders will emerge in the inmate groups found in restrictive organizational climates; relatively cooperative and positive leaders will emerge in the inmate groups found in permissive organizational climates.*

Hypothesis 5f *Inmates will tend to choose as leaders other inmates who are similar to themselves in terms of various personal, offense, and organizational characteristics.*

Hypothesis 5g *Inmates will tend to limit their choices of leaders to inmates who are similar to themselves in terms of personal, offense, and organizational characteristics more often in restrictive organizational climates than in permissive organizational climates.*

Hypothesis 5h *Inmates will tend to choose as leaders other inmates who hold normative orientations similar to their own.*

A certain minimal length of stay in the institution will be a prerequisite for leadership status, and in general leaders will be found among the inmates who have been in the institution for a longer period of time. A certain amount of time is required for the potential leader to establish himself as a leader, to obtain knowledge of the institution, to obtain control over various kinds of resources, and to obtain influence over his fellow inmates.

We predict that age will be directly related to leadership status in institutions for juveniles and youths; leaders will generally be older than nonleaders. This relationship will not hold, however, in institutions for adults. Among juveniles and youths, increasing age generally means increasing knowledge, experience, size, and strength. Young inmates who may differ in age by only a few years may differ substantially on these characteristics. After a certain age, however, the rate at which one continues to grow in these areas levels off, and a difference in years no longer translates into an advantage. In terms of physical strength it may mean a disadvantage. For these reasons we believe that age will be related to leadership status in institutions for juveniles and youths, but not in institutions for adults.

Hypothesis 5c states that inmate leaders will have more education than nonleaders. We believe that education will be related to leadership status for two reasons. First, education provides the inmate with knowledge and skills he can use to an advantage in dealing with his fellow inmates and institutional staff. Secondly, the fact that an inmate has completed more formal education can be seen as an indicator of his ability to "work the system."

Hypothesis 5d posits a relationship between leadership status and offense history. This hypothesis is based primarily on previous studies of the correlates of leadership status in correctional institutions. Grusky and Berk reported that inmates who had committed crimes against persons rather than public order or property crimes were disproportionately represented among inmate leaders.[7] Clemmer, Schrag, and Berk all reported that the inmate leaders in their studies had more extensive offense records than nonleaders.[8] An explanation for this relationship depends heavily on the meaning one is willing to assign to the inmate's offense history. Can it be taken as an indicator of his past and future behavior? Should it be viewed as a measure of the inmate's experience in dealing with the criminal justice system? At this point we prefer to defer the discussion of these points and will address them later when we examine the relationship of offense history as an independent variable in relation to various dependent variables. Given the weight of previous findings, however, we do predict a relationship between offense history and leadership status.

Our Hypothesis 5e, regarding the types of inmate leaders who will emerge, is based on the same premises underlying our earlier hypotheses regarding the general character of the inmate system and the friendship relationships that would emerge. A restrictive organizational climate results in a setting in which even legitimate gratifications are severely limited; the distance between staff and inmates is great; the rules are standardized and allow little discretion on the part of the inmates. The restrictive climate will provide a reservoir of alienation between the inmates and staff, and it will be those inmates who are willing to violate institutional rules to increase and reallocate scarce resources who will be able to assume leadership in the inmate group. Gratifications will be severely limited under the prevailing institutional order; inmates who are willing to violate that order will at the very least have greater control over their distribution and use. In the permissive organizational setting the social distance between staff and inmates is much smaller; gratifications are obtainable to a much greater extent through legitimate channels; the inmates have little to gain by informal adaptations that contravene the established order of the institution. It is on this basis, then, that we predict that the restrictive organizational setting will be conducive to the emergence of uncooperative and negative leaders, while the permissive organizational setting will be conducive to the emergence of cooperative and positive inmate leaders.

We have stated in Hypothesis 5f that inmates will tend to recognize and follow leaders who are similar to themselves in terms of various personal, offense, and organizational characteristics. Inmates are more likely to acknowledge as leaders other inmates who are like themselves and are likely to represent their interests and lead the way in obtaining those things which they themselves seek. Certain personal, offense, and organizational characteristics serve as indicators of those interests. We therefore expect inmates to choose as leaders other inmates who are similar to themselves in terms of these indicators. Schrag, one of the few researchers to have examined this point in a correctional setting, found that inmates tended to choose as leaders other inmates who were similar to themsleves in terms of ethnic background, intelligence, number of previous offenses, nature of offense, sentence, institutional adjustment, and pathological psychological diagnosis.[9]

In line with our earlier arguments regarding the structuring of friendship choices, we predict that this tendency to choose leaders from "amongst one's own" will be more dominant in restrictive organizational settings than in permissive organizational settings (Hypothesis 5g). Leadership choices will be more structured along categorical lines in restrictive organizational climates, much the same way that we have predicted friendship choices will be.

In Hypothesis 5h we predict that inmates will tend to recognize and follow as leaders other inmates who hold attitudes, values, and beliefs similar to their own. The leader of a group serves as a symbol and embodiment of the attitudes, values, and beliefs of the group. To the extent that the inmates identify leaders whom they would choose to represent them or whom they see as exercising a desirable influence, the inmates will select leaders who hold beliefs similar to their own.

Summary

We have used the model of the alternate society as an umbrella concept to present a consistent set of hypotheses regarding variables affecting the prisonized versus nonprisonized adaptations of the inmates, the integration of the inmates into the inmate group, integration and inmate orientations, interpersonal relationships among the inmates, and leadership patterns within the inmate group. Some of these hypotheses are directly derivable from the model of the alternate society and constitute a test of the central propositions of the model. Other hypotheses, while not derived directly from the model, are consistent with it and allow us to round out the portrait of the inmate system.

We turn now to Chapter 3 and a discussion of the two research sites Federal East and Federal West, their staffs and inmates, and their location within our model of the alternate society.

Notes

1. Stanton Wheeler, "Socialization in Correctional Communities," *American Sociological Review* 26 (1961): 697-712; Peter G. Garabedian, "Social Roles and Processes of Socialization in the Prison Community," *Social Problems* 11 (1963): 139-152; and Daniel Glaser, *The Effectiveness of a Prison and Parole System* (Indianapolis: Bobbs-Merrill Co., 1964), pp. 90-98.

2. Robert C. Atchley and Patrick M. McCabe, "Socialization in Correctional Communities: A Replication," *American Sociological Review* 33 (1968): 774-785.

3. David Street, Robert Vinter, and Charles Perrow, *Organization for Treatment* (New York: The Free Press, 1966), pp. 230-238.

4. Glaser, *Effectiveness of a Prison System*, pp. 111-117; Rosemary C. Sarri, "Organizational Patterns and Client Perspectives in Juvenile Correctional Institutions: A Comparative Study" (Ph.D. dissertation, University of Michigan, 1962), p. 200; Clarence C. Schrag, "Leadership among Prison Inmates," *American Sociological Review* 19 (1954): 37-42; and Stanton Wheeler, "Social Organization in a Correctional Community" (Ph.D. dissertation, University of Washington, 1958), pp. 65-87.

5. John Irwin, "The Prison Experience: The Convict World," in *Correctional Institutions*, ed. Robert Carter, Daniel Glaser, and Leslie T. Wilkins, (Philadelphia: J.B. Lippincott Co., 1972), pp. 173-192.

6. Cecil A. Gibb, "Leadership," in *Handbook of Social Psychology*, ed. Gardner Lindzey and Elliot Aronson, (Reading, Mass.: Addison-Wesley Publishing Co., 1969), 2d ed., vol. 4, p. 226.

7. Oscar Grusky, "Treatment Goals and Organizational Behavior: A Study of an Experimental Prison Camp" (Ph.D. dissertation, University of Michigan, 1957), pp. 180-181; and Bernard Berk, "Informal Social Organization and Leadership among Inmates in Treatment and Custodial Prisons: A Comparative Study" (Ph.D. dissertation, University of Michigan, 1962), pp. 119-120.

8. Donald Clemmer, *The Prison Community* (New York: Holt, Rinehart and Winston, 1958), pp. 134-148; Schrag, "Leadership among Prison Inmates," p. 40; and Berk, "Informal Social Organization among Inmates," pp. 119-120.

9. Schrag, "Leadership among Prison Inmates," p. 41.

3

The Research Settings: Organizational Climates and Inmate Background Characteristics

The data to be used in examining the hypotheses discussed in Chapter 2 are drawn from a larger study of correctional programs conducted by Professors Rosemary Sarri and Robert Vinter of the University of Michigan School of Social Work and funded by the U.S. Bureau of Prisons.[1] Extensive data are available for two federal correctional institutions for young offenders, Federal East and Federal West.

At the time of the study, Federal East was a recently opened federal youth center with a population capacity of approximately 325 and a current population of 176. The physical plant was new and modern; the program design for the inmates was complex and innovative. It included an institutionwide differential classification and treatment program and token economy system. The inmates ranged in age from 15-22, with a median age of 19.3; they were mostly whites with a minority of blacks and a small number of Indians; most of the inmates (62 percent) had been convicted of an interstate auto theft violation. Selection criteria excluded from the initial population offenders who had been in a federal institution previously or who had a history of escapes, assaultive behavior, or homosexual behavior.

Federal West was the western counterpart of Federal East. It had a population capacity of approximately 325 inmates, and a current population of 312. Its physical plant was over twenty-five years old; its program can be described as "traditional," with emphasis on high school education or vocational training, generally in combination with institutional maintenance work details. The inmates were of the same median age as those at Federal East; here also most of the inmates were whites, but there was also a sizeable minority of Indians and smaller minorities of black and Spanish-American inmates. The largest single offense category at Federal West also involved violation of an interstate auto theft statute (47 percent). While there are some differences between the two inmate populations, i.e., the larger proportion of Indians at Federal West and the possible exclusion of certain types of inmates at Federal East, it is felt that the similarities outweigh the differences and that the two populations are comparable for most purposes. The major differences between Federal East and Federal West were at the organizational level: a permissive institutional climate prevailed at Federal East, while a relatively restrictive institutional climate was a characteristic of Federal West.

Data on the organization, staff, and inmates of the two institutions were obtained from organizational documents, direct observations of the staffs and inmates, interviews with executives, staff, and inmates, questionnaires administered to staff and inmates, inmate files, and from the inmate data bank maintained by the Federal Bureau of Prisons research office. As part of the larger study, questionnaires were administered to the staff and inmates at Federal East at three points in time: Survey I, at the opening of the institution; Survey II, eight months later; and Survey III, fourteen months subsequent to the opening of the institution. Survey II was the most extensive data survey, and inmate file data were abstracted from the institution's records at that time. Administration of the questionnaires and file abstraction activities were carried out at Federal West approximately a month prior to the execution of Survey II activities at Federal East. The data from this survey, Survey II, and the file abstraction constitute the main basis of our analysis in the following chapters.

Organizational documents, observations, interviews, and staff and inmate questionnaires provide us with measures of the institutional climates that prevailed at each of the institutions. The inmate questionnaires also provide adequate data to permit construction of indices designed to measure inmate attitudes toward the institution and staff, the degree of inmate prisonization, and the extent to which a condition of "pluralistic ignorance" regarding other inmates' normative orientations existed in the inmate populations. In addition, the questionnaires also contain sociometric questions and leadership identifications, which allow a partial reconstruction of the friendship and leadership structures at the two institutions. The file data contain numerous variables regarding institutional adjustment (e.g., disciplinary reports, times in segregation, etc.) as well as extensive background information (age, race, education, etc.), which can be utilized as valuable descriptive information and as control variables in analyzing the relationships hypothesized in the preceding chapter.

The Deprivation Model and Organizational Climates

In the deprivation model of prisonization the inmate group is viewed as a system oriented toward ameliorating its members' deprivation. The form and normative content of the inmate system significantly is affected by the environmental contingencies or organizational climate the inmates encounter. The main variable affecting the alternate society of inmates is the organizational climate within which the inmates must live and attempt to meet their physical, psychological, and social needs. By organizational climate we are referring to the total organizational atmosphere or milieu confronting the inmates provided by the physical setting, organizational goals, program components, staff attitudes, and other aspects of institutional life. These variations in turn are related to variations in the responses of the inmates to the institutional experience.

While there are a number of dimensions along which we might characterize organizational climates, our concern with the immediate contingencies of everyday life facing the inmates leads us to focus on a dimension that is perhaps best characterized as one of permissiveness-restrictiveness. Correctional institutions vary in the degree of permission-restriction imposed on the inmates in terms of material gratifications and deprivations and decisionmaking power. In some institutions the inmates face a relatively favorable balance of gratifications and deprivations and are allowed a good deal of decisionmaking power regarding their institutional programs, daily schedules, and personal associations. We would label such institutions as having relatively permissive climates. In other institutions the inmates face a relatively unfavorable balance of gratifications and deprivations and are allowed to make only a very limited number of decisions if any at all. We would label such institutions as having relatively restrictive climates. A particular institution can be typed by placement on this hypothetical continuum of permission-restriction, and the character of the alternate society of inmates will be related to the location of the institution on this continuum.

Previous research on correctional institutions utilizing a goal model of analysis demonstrated a strong correlation both between treatment goals and what we have here termed permissive organizational climates and be tween custodial goals and what we have here termed restrictive organizational climates.[2] The approach taken here, while not identical with the goal model, is congruent with and supportive of it. Organizational goals are seen as being a major but not sole determinant of organizational climates. Other factors such as environmental constraints, resource levels, interorganizational ties, staff backgrounds, etc. may also have an important impact on the climate that prevails at a particular institution. Our analysis will begin with certain given types of organizational climates; we will examine their impact on the alternate society of inmates, recognizing that there are a number of variables that influence the organizational climate.

Through the comparison of the physical plants, goals, program components, staff, and staff attitudes, it can be seen that Federal East had a relatively permissive organizational climate, while Federal West presented a relatively restrictive organizational climate.[3]

The Physical Settings

Federal East was a newly opened federal minimum security institution for youthful offenders. It was located in a rural border state near a small city of approximately 30,000 people. Its physical plant was attractive, modern, and relatively costly, having cost eleven million dollars to construct. There were no fences, bars, or other visible security features, and the one-story brick buildings on well-landscaped grounds nestled in a small valley more closely resembled a college campus than a correctional institution. The inmates were housed in five cottages, each of which had a capacity of sixty residents, and a smaller reception cottage. The cottages were all very similar in design, with a large recreation and lounge area with cathedral ceilings and a fireplace, separate offices for caseworkers and counselors, and three different types of rooms for the inmates, ranging from semiprivate cubicles to private rooms with their own washroom facilities. In addition there was a segregation cottage with a capacity of thirty inmates that served as a maximum security unit for the institution. Other facilities included a very attractive interdenominational chapel, a modern education and tràining center, and several other buildings that housed other institutional services such as administration, food service, and laundry. The education building included facilities for academic instruction, general vocational training, and recreation. Included in the recreation facilities were an auditorium, a gymnasium, and an Olympic-sized swimming pool.

Federal West was an older federal minimum security institution for youthful offenders built about thirty years prior to the time of this study. It was located in a semirural area approximately a mile from a large metropolitan center. Physically, Federal West resembled a traditional custodial institution. It was surrounded by a cyclone fence topped with several strands of barbed wire and an alarm wire. There were three guard towers located along the perimeter of the institution; during the daylight hours unarmed guards conducted continuous surveillance of the perimeter from the vantage points of the towers. The main complex of buildings was put together in the shape of a rectangle with a large courtyard in the center. On the east and west sides of the rectangle were the main living units, upper east and lower east and upper west and lower west. Each of the four main living units held between sixty and seventy-five inmates in two types of living arrangements: a large open dormitory setting in which most of the inmates resided and a series of small individual rooms. Also in the living unit or connected to it was a small recreation room and several very small rooms used as offices by the counselors. Opportunities for privacy in this setting were noticeably absent. In addition to the main living units there were also several smaller, special-purpose living units in which the inmates assigned to work release, intensive treatment, and segregation resided. Administrative offices and a chapel were toward the front of the complex, while the dining and food services and a recreation room, euphemistically referred to as a gymnasium, made up the back of the rectangle. Connected to the back of the complex and off to the side was the building that housed the educational and vocational training facilities. Although clean, the buildings were generally unattractive; and institutional green, which seemed to be the prevailing color, reflected the tone of the institution.

Organizational Goals

While there are a number of arguments concerning the limitations of a goal model of organizational analysis, the analysis of organizational goals is essential to a comprehensive understanding of organizational behavior.

Goals serve a number of important functions in correctional institutions as in all organizational settings. These include: (1) establishing priorities for resource allocations; (2) delimiting the range of technologies available to the organization; (3) legitimating the organization's claim to resources; (4) providing an ideological base for the recruitment and motivation of staff; (5) providing standards for the elevation of organizational effectiveness and/or efficiency; and (6) facilitating or impeding organizational innovation and change. In even more basic terms, organizational goals denote the purposes of the organization; in people-changing organizations such as correctional institutions, the goals denote the changes to be brought about in their raw materials, i.e. the inmates. Implicit in such goal statements are beliefs concerning the raw materials—their pasts, their present condition, and their potential for the future. Organizational goals, technologies, and structures are interrelated and interact to produce distinctive patterns of organizational behavior. If certain goals are to be pursued, some technologies will be more effective than others in attaining those goals; certain organizational structures will be more appropriate than others for implementing those technologies. The technologies and structures utilized will play a fundamental role in determining the actions staff will take vis-à-vis the inmates and the degree of autonomy and extent of material comforts the inmates may legitimately enjoy. Thus, organizational goals, especially those that are actually subscribed to and operationalized by the organizational personnel, have a major impact on the nature of the organizational climate that prevails at the institution, especially in terms of the permissive-restrictive character of that climate. With this in mind, let us briefly turn to a review of the formal goals of Federal East and Federal West and to the staffs' perceptions of the goals that were actually implemented at the two institutions.

A rather lengthy and elaborate statement of formal goals existed at Federal East.[4] The actual statement of the organization's goals included one primary goal and seven subgoals with a total of nineteen subsections. The primary goal of the institution was to:

Provide for the care, custody and treatment of committed youthful offenders so that the greatest number of these individuals are returned to the community to lead nondelinquent lives.

This statement designates the product goal or end state desired: the maximization of the number of offenders who will go on to "lead nondelinquent lives." Federal East's subgoals are also of relevance to our discussion here, since they denote the process goals or means by which the organization seeks to attain its product goal. The first three of these subgoals refer to treatment and have considerable bearing on the organizational climate seen as appropriate to treatment:

1. Establish an institutional environment where growth and positive changes in students will take place.
2. Develop a classification system which will identify and direct the proper student to .he most appropriate treatment programs.
3. Provide specific treatment to meet individual student needs.

Subgoal 4 refers to custodial concerns, subgoals 5 and 6 refer to community relations, and subgoal 7 focuses on evaluation of the overall program. Overall, the subgoals reflect a relatively heavy emphasis on treatment and recognize the necessity of an environment conducive to treatment. One of the objectives given under subgoal 1 is even more explicit on this particular point:

d. Develop constructive staff-to-staff, student-to-student and staff-to-student relationships, which are the primary vehicles for change, by providing an open communications system.

This objective represents the explicit intent to replace the prisonization phenomenon with constructive relationships among the staff and inmates of the institution.

In marked contrast to Federal East, Federal West had no written formal goal statement. Statements of the director of Federal West and staff activities indicated that priority was given to training and custody over other goals. Treatment and the requisite environment for treatment appeared to receive much less emphasis. Our observers concluded that the product goal of Federal West was better-trained and better-educated inmates, and the process goals through which this was to be achieved were the establishment and maintenance of appropriate training and custody programs.

Official goals often tend to be stated in relatively vague and general terms, often represent the intentions and perceptions of the organizational elite, and, in some cases, represent earlier goals rather than current goals, since the mandate and domain of the organization may change while the formal written statements remain unrevised. Therefore to overcome the weaknesses inherent in an analysis based on a statement of official goals and to measure the operative goals of the two institutions as they were perceived by the staff, a detailed questionnaire was developed. This instrument was based on the technique previously used by Gross for measuring goals in university settings.[5] The instrument was designed so as to elicit from the respondents indications of how important they thought that goal should be. Since we are interested in what goals were being stressed at a certain point in time, we will focus here only on "how important" staff thought particular goals were at the time of our study.[6]

Staff were asked to respond to items in four general categories: staff-institution relationships, staff-inmate relationships, institution-community relations, and desired changes in inmates. Responses to these items were then processed using a factor analysis, and scores were computed for each factor. The result was five factors: (1) a staff decisionmaking-morale factor, (2) a treatment-community factor, (3) an education-training factor, (4) a custody-control factor, and (5) a rehabilitative goal factor.

The staffs at both institutions felt that education-training was the most important goal. Both staffs saw this goal receiving the most emphasis at their institutions. Beyond this, however, there was a distinct divergence in the reports. The staff at Federal East reported that treatment-community and rehabilitation concerns were next most important and ranked above custody-control in terms of emphasis. At Federal West custody-control was the second most stressed objective, ranking ahead of both treatment-community and rehabilitation goals.

The significance of this differential ranking for the organizational climate, which the inmate must confront, becomes evident if we examine the items that comprise the treatment-community factor, the rehabilitation factor, and the custody-control factor.

Treatment-Community Factor
1. To encourage volunteer work at the institution.
2. To develop ties with universities and social agencies.
3. To work for the acceptance of the institution in the community.
4. To establish close relationships with inmates.
5. To provide models of behavior for inmates.
6. To keep inmates satisfied and content.

Rehabilitation Factor
1. To develop good social habits.
2. To develop emotional maturity.
3. To develop a capacity to cope with everyday problems.
4. To develop respect for the law.

Custody-Control Factor
1. To maintain order and discipline.
2. To prevent escapes.
3. To protect the local community from inmates.

The greater emphasis on keeping inmates satisfied and content, establishing close relationships with the inmates, and building ties with outsiders for the benefit of the inmates indicated that a more permissive organizational climate was purposely being sought at Federal East; on the other hand, the greater emphasis at Federal West on maintaining order and discipline, preventing escapes, and protecting the community denotes efforts to maintain a much more restrictive organizational climate.

Program Components

Program components have major implications for the quality of the organizational climate of an institution. On the one hand, components that result in the expenditure of resources in certain ways and that shape staff-inmate and inmate-inmate relations will have a direct impact on social relations and the balance of permissiveness and restrictiveness prevailing at the institution; on the other hand, certain program components require as preconditons for their implementation a particular kind of organizational climate and a particular kind of social structure. In this section we will compare and contrast the major program components at Federal East and Federal West and examine their implications for the balance of gratifications and deprivations presented to the inmates and their implications for the social relationships that emerged at the two institutions.

Classification Systems. The complex of programs at Federal East included a number of relatively sophisticated and intricate components. Perhaps the most significant of these was the differential treatment program. This program was based on a typology of behavior categories developed by Dr. Herbert Quay. Individual inmates were assigned to one of five categories on the basis of the results of: (1) a forty-four item checklist of behavior problems completed by a corrections officer in the admissions cottage, (2) a one-hundred item true-false, self-report questionnaire completed by the inmate, and (3) a thirty-six item checklist based on an analysis of the inmate's life history completed by a caseworker. The behavior categories (BCs) and the primary dimensions on which they were based were: BC-1, inadequate-immature; BC-2, neurotic-conflicted; BC-3, unsocialized aggressive or psychopathic; BC-4, socialized or subcultural delinquent; and BC-5, a subgroup of the BC-1 (inadequate) and BC-4 (subcultural) groups. Each BC group was housed in its own cottage and subject to a general treatment strategy deemed appropriate to meet the needs of that particular group. In addition, an attempt was also made to staff each cottage with personnel who had the appropriate dispositions and skills to work most effectively with the various kinds of youth. (Original plans called for the testing and classification of staff members, but union regulations prevented this. Assignments were eventually made on the basis of self-preferences and supervisors' recommendations.) Within the cottage, an individualized program was developed by the inmate and a cottage treatment team consisting of a caseworker, a representative of the educational department, and a corrections officer.

The differential treatment program had several important implications for our research questions. The program provided for the identification of particular factors that contributed to the offender's delinquent behavior—inadequacy, neuroticism, psychopathology, socialization—and also provided guidelines for treating groups of inmates. Among the prescriptions were those dealing with the extent to which inmates were to be supported, given freedom to express themselves, or closely controlled. Thus we find that a primary objective in working with the BC-1s "is to establish a secure, non-threatening environment" and "activities should be oriented around taking personal responsibility for oneself."[7] In contrast, the treatment strategies for the BC-3s were to "focus first on controlling them so that they may benefit more from all treatment programs. This necessitates meeting their needs in a highly structured environment."[8] In addition, the treatment strategies seen as appropriate for each BC group emphasized different staff-inmate and inmate-inmate relations. Individual counseling, physical activities, and large cottage meetings were the different strategies that were seen as appropriate for different cottages. Thus, we would expect the differential treatment program to have had an impact on the inmate's reaction to the institution and his involvement in social relationships within the institution.

At Federal West there was no equivalent differential classification and treatment program. On entering the institution inmates were immediately placed into one of the four main living units. This assignment was done on a simple rotation basis. The inmates were then given a battery of standard psychological and academic tests and "classified" in terms of their level of functioning. All living units were subject to essentially the same institutional routines. The major exceptions to this were the special living units: the work release unit, the Intensive Treatment Unit (I.T.U.), and the segregation unit. The work release unit housed inmates who were close to release and who were on work release or study release. Supervision was generally more relaxed there than in the regular units. The Intensive Treatment Unit was for inmates who needed more intensive supervision and counseling than they could receive in the regular units. Attention was given

45329

to inmates on an individualized basis. The segregation unit was used primarily for disciplinary and custodial purposes. Thus, while we did find a rudimentary classification system, it was based on the degree of trouble the inmate presented to the institution or on the inmate's prerelease status rather than an explicit treatment rationale.

Rewards and Reinforcements. An institutionwide token economy system and a system of class privileges constituted two major sources of rewards available to all the inmates at Federal East. Through the token economy system—an approach based on operant conditioning principles of behavior modification—inmates earned points, which could be used to purchase privileges and goods both inside and outside of the institution. The inmates received points for good behavior and the attainment of performance goals in school, on work details, and in the cottages. The token economy system was routinized on an institutionwide basis, and the inmates received weekly computer-processed "paychecks." When it was first implemented, however, it was thought that it would be easier to process the token economy data if points were subtracted rather than added. Consequently, the system as put into effect was originally a system of punishments rather than rewards. This was eventually reversed but not until after it had been in effect for eight months. It was possible for an inmate to earn up to 750 points or the equivalent of $7.50 plus a small additional sum through bonus points, which were issued on an irregular spontaneous basis for positive behavior. Although the inmate's earnings were subject to (infrequent) fines for misbehavior, a small income tax, deductions for room rental and release savings (mandatory for certain classes of inmates), the net income was enough to produce what one staff member at the institution described as "an economy of abundance." The inmates could regularly purchase cigarettes and personal items at the institution's commissary, and a snack bar was open in the cottage on a nightly basis providing the inmates with an opportunity to purchase items such as soda, potato chips, candy, etc. The program operated in such a way that all the inmates had some income every week, and the majority were regularly earning close to the maximum number of points possible.

Closely linked to the token economy system at Federal East was a system of class levels—trainee, apprentice, honor—which existed in all cottages. The inmate's class level determined the number and kinds of privileges he enjoyed in the institution. The higher the class level, the higher the rate of token economy point earnings, the fewer points the inmate was required to save, the better his living quarters, the later his lights-out time, etc. Honor status was a prerequisite for a parole hearing.

In sum, what we found at Federal East was a purposeful attempt to structure the institutional environment to facilitate the achievment of program goals; one of the net results was a relatively comfortable setting in which goods and services that are generally absent in a correctional institution were fairly readily accessible to the inmates. Especially in comparison with other institutional settings, the inmates at Federal East enjoyed "an economy of abundance."

At Federal West also it was possible for inmates to earn cash awards through a program known as Meritorious Service Awards (MSA). An inmate who had been in the institution at least ninety days and on a certain work detail for at least sixty days was eligible to receive MSA on the recommendation of the detail supervisor. Initially the inmate received $10.00 a month MSA, but it was possible for the inmate to earn up to $25.00. Inmates could earn as much as $5.00 a month MSA in vocational training courses; each academic course completed was worth approximately $6.00; a G.E.D. certificate earned the inmate $15.00; and a high school diploma was worth $25.00. While theoretically MSA might have been a source of income for many inmates, this does not appear to have been the case. In informal interviews a number of inmates scoffed at the MSA program claiming that few, if any, benefited from it. Open-ended projective questions on our inmate questionnaire elicited a number of responses indicating many inmates were not receiving their MSA payments and that those who were receiving it were getting it late or in very small amounts. Further, an examination of the institution's own records indicated that only 29 of the 312 inmates were actually scheduled to receive monthly MSA awards. In sum, only a small proportion of the inmates at Federal West received any form of MSA, and most inmates had to rely on relatives and friends outside the institution to supply them with commissary funds. In contrast to the "economy of abundance" that prevailed at Federal East, the inmates at Federal West experienced "an economy of scarcity" in which "two for one rackets"[a] flourished and inmates "pressured" other inmates to share or hand over outright their commissary.

The terms *economy of abundance* and *economy of scarcity* sum up rather succinctly the conditions faced by the inmates at Federal East and Federal West respectively. In the former institution we found most of the inmates earning close to the maximum number of token economy points possible, the equivalent of approximately $32.50 a month. At the latter institution we found only a small proportion—less than 10 percent of the inmates—earning any MSA at all. Even the maximum MSA—$25.00 a month—which was earned by only a few, was less than the maximum in token economy points that an inmate at Federal East could earn.

---

[a]In the "two for one" arrangement an inmate lends cigarettes or other commissary to another inmate who is required to pay back the lender at a rate of two for one by a certain date. If the borrower cannot make the repayment within the specified period of time, the amount owed doubles and keeps doubling at the expiration of each loan period.

While Federal West did not have a formal system of class levels with corresponding kinds of privileges as was found at Federal East, it did have a system of custody classification—minimum, medium, close—which specified the degree of supervision that should be maintained over each inmate. Key staff saw the custody classification as an administrative categorization used to minimize the likelihood of escapes and not to be used as a reward or punishment; reportedly an inmate could get parole while on close custody just as easily as an inmate on medium or minimum custody.

The contrasts in the prevailing climates in terms of the level of gratifications available to the inmates can perhaps best be conveyed by the inmates' reactions to the researchers' promises to give them "cokes and chips" after they had completed questionnaires. The reactions of the inmates at both institutions were relatively subdued, but for distinctly different reasons. For the inmates at Federal East this treat was nothing special. On the other hand, the inmates at Federal West were skeptical, and many would not believe that they would be given anything. After they had received the promised treats they went out of their way to thank the researchers. The manner in which these treats were distributed also indicates the prevailing climate at the two institutions. At Federal East a cottage officer opened the snack bar and yelled, "Snack bar's open." and proceeded to hand out the treats. At Federal West all the inmates were assembled in the "big yard" and marched through a gate into the "little yard." Corrrections officers at the gate handed each inmate an opened can of soda (unopened cans were seen as dangerous weapons) and a bag of potato chips.

Discipline and Control Measures. A number of discipline and control techniques were available to the staff at both Federal East and Federal West. Control measures at Federal East included: use of a "time out room;" minor disciplinary reports which could lead to token economy fines or a loss of privileges; major disciplinary reports which could result in demotion in class level, placement in the security unit, or disciplinary transfer to another institution; and the forfeiture of the inmate's institutional savings, in the event of escape or disciplinary transfer. The organizational manual at Federal East provided the following guideline for the utilization of these penalties:

In imposing these control measures, the guiding principle will be that strong punishment leads to the perpetrator being viewed as a hero by his peers. Therefore, emphasis is placed on mild forms of control.[9]

At Federal West the discipline and control measures and guidelines for this use were less formally enunciated. Disciplinary measures included: use of the stairwells as time out facilities; minor misconduct reports ("pinkies") which could result in the loss of privileges or the assignment of extra work chores in the dorm; and major disciplinary reports ("white sheets") which could result in withheld or forfeited good-time, placement in the segregation unit, or disciplinary transfer to another institution. There was no officially promulgated policy regarding the utilization of these sanctions, and their use seemed to vary considerably among staff members.

While at Federal East there appeared to be an attempt to integrate and coordinate disciplinary actions with other aspects of the institutional program so as not to impede rehabilitation efforts, this did not appear to be the case at Federal West. Disciplinary actions constituted a separate sphere of operations, which often took precedence over other aspects of the program, e.g., an inmate who had good-time withheld or forfeited was not eligible for certain privileges or program changes until he had earned back the good-time lost.

Counseling Programs. Counseling activities were a routine part of the daily schedule at Federal East, and regular time slots were allotted for counseling activities in the daily schedule of each cottage. While the amount and form of the counseling varied from cottage to cottage, each inmate received a minimum of two to three hours of counseling per week. The various forms the counseling activities took included individual counseling, modeling, roleplaying, psychodrama, sociodrama, guided discussion groups, and cottage forum meetings. Both caseworkers and counselors (corrections officers) were assigned caseloads of inmates to counsel. Interaction of the professional caseworkers and the corrections staff and inmates was facilitated by the caseworker's position as cottage supervisor and the physical location of his office in the cottage. The two chaplains at Federal East also provided spiritual counseling, although a good part of their time was spent organizing and running the Life School Program in which volunteers from the community came to the institution to visit and spend time with the inmates.

Provisions were also made for counseling activities at Federal West, although on a more limited basis. Counseling there most often took the form of an hour-long group session once a week. Almost all the counseling was done by corrections officers, and caseworkers had but limited direct contact with the inmates. Several of these counselors had apparently, on their own initiative, established special counseling groups for Indians, Spanish-Americans, and drug offenders in an effort to meet the special needs of these inmates. More frequent and intensive counseling was provided for the inmates in the Intensive Treatment Unit, and a number of inmates acknowledged that this was the best and most helpful counseling program in the institution. Spiritual counseling was provided by several chaplains and chaplain trainees at Federal West. While there was a larger number of chaplains at Federal West, the scope of their activities was somewhat more limited than those of the chaplains at Federal East, who were actively engaged in linking the institution with the community. On the whole, Federal West placed less emphasis on counseling than did Federal East, as measured in terms of the amount of time set aside for such activities, the number of staff assigned to counseling, and the amount and kind of training given to the counseling staff.

Education: Academic and Vocational. The education program was one of the key program components at both Federal East and Federal West. At Federal East each inmate was scheduled to spend three out of four daytime program periods—approximately six hours—in some form of academic or vocational training. The education program at Federal East was broken down into three basic areas: (1) industrial training; (2) supportive education; and (3) social, cultural, intellectual, and physical education—otherwise known as the SCIP program. The industrial training program, which was divided into four vocational clusters (aerospace, graphic arts, electronics, and technical services), was designed to provide inmates with the basic knowledge and requisite skills of a particular area rather than producing highly trained technicians. The supportive education program was to provide students with the academic skills needed to work in the various vocational areas, while the SCIP program was designed to help the inmate develop the social, cultural, intellectual, and physical skills necessary to get along with his fellow workers and operate on a satisfactory level in society. In addition to these three basic programs, there was a remedial education program, a program to prepare students to obtain the G.E.D. (high school equivalency degree), and a college prep program.

At Federal East institutional work details were limited to approximately 1.5 hours per day and were identified as "chores;" inmates performed very few of the key tasks necessary for the operation and maintenance of the institution.

At Federal West the education program was seen as the most important part of the overall program of the institution. Here the inmate's day was divided into two half-day modules (morning and afternoon), and the inmate generally spent a half day on a work detail assignment and a half day in academic or vocational training. At the time of our survey about 20 percent of the population were assigned to a full-day of work details, 30 percent were assigned to a full-day of academic and/or vocational training activities, and 50 percent were assigned to a full-day combination of work detail and academic and vocational training activities. The academic program consisted of courses in four main areas: language arts and communication skills, social science concepts and values, scientific knowledge and attitudes, computational abilities and information. There was no college preparatory program. Raising the educational level of the inmates, providing remedial instruction, preparing inmates for the G.E.D. exams, and providing the supportive education necessary for vocational training were all features of the Federal West education program. There were nine basic vocational training courses, e.g., auto-mechanics, auto body, welding, woodworking, machine shop, etc. In addition, a number of the work details provided experiences that both staff and inmates recognized as valuable, although their main function was to provide the manpower necessary to operate and maintain the physical plant.

Staff: Structure, Characteristics, and Perspectives

A very significant aspect of the environment with which the inmate must cope is that of the staff. The official staff roles and the perspectives held by the staff will strongly influence the ways in which the inmates are handled, and the orientation of the staff toward the inmates may be seen as part of the balance of gratifications and deprivations the inmates must face. In this section we will compare the organizational structure and staff roles that existed at the two institutions, the characteristics of the staff, and the perspectives that the staff held regarding the inmates and the kinds of care, custody, and treatment they should receive.

Staff Structure. The structuring of staff roles involves the allocation of responsibility and authority over all aspects of institutional life. The investment of decisionmaking authority in certain staff groups will determine which professional ideologies will predominate in the day-to-day operations of the institution and will have profound impact on the prevailing organizational climate. In the discussion of staff structure we will limit our consideration mainly to those segments of the staff who were most involved with the inmates on a day-by-day basis, the treatment and corrections staffs.

At Federal East the staff were assigned to four major departments: Business, Medical, Education, and Case Management, each headed by a supervisor who reported to the assistant director and through him to the director. The most significant difference in staff structure between Federal East and Federal West (as well as between Federal East and most other federal correctional institutions) existed in the relationship between the treatment and corrections departments. At Federal East the treatment and corrections departments, which were traditionally distinct and separate in Bureau of Prisons institutions, were integrated into a single department of Case Management. Not only was there structural integration at the department level with the two departments combined under a single supervisor, a professional caseworker, but also integration took place at the cottage level where professional caseworkers supervised correctional staff.

Further, the caseworker cottage supervisor was administratively and physically located within the cottage, making supervision of cottage counselors and cottage correctional officers more effective and enabling him to be actively involved in the everyday affairs of the cottage.

The cottage supervisor, a caseworker, and his assistant, a correctional supervisor, were responsible for all cottage activity including program planning and implementation and the supervision of other staff. In addition they carried counseling caseloads in the cottage. Working under the supervision of the cottage supervisor and the assistant cottage supervisor were the correctional counselors, whose main responsibilities involved the implementation of treatment programs and counseling activities. In addition, there were cottage officers who were primarily responsible for order and cleanliness in the cottages.

At Federal West the staff were divided into ten separate departments, each headed by a supervisor who reported directly to the associate director and through him to the director: Classification and Parole, Personnel, Safety, Education, Chaplains, Mechanical, Corrections, Administration, Food, and Medical. The department charged with treatment activities, the department of Classification and Parole, and the Corrections department were distinct and separate departments. The Classification and Parole department, composed mainly of professional caseworkers providing casework services to the inmates, was physically and organizationally separate from the cottages and had little if anything to say about the day-to-day activities in the cottages. The caseworkers had offices in the administration building, met with the inmates on an individual basis, participated in treatment team conferences, and reported directly to the head of the Classification and Parole department, who in turn reported directly to the associate director and director of the institution. The Corrections department handled all inmate custody and control activities, including all cottage activities. The cottage officers and correctional counselors reported to the cottage supervisor (a senior corrections officer), who in turn reported to the operational correctional supervisors and through them to the chief correctional supervisor, who in turn was responsible to the associate director and director of the institution. All corrections staff, inside and outside of the cottages, were more or less under the direct control of the chief correctional supervisor. The primary focus of the activities of the Corrections department was the maintenance of custody and control. Corrections counselors were involved in counseling activities on only a limited basis, and there were no other treatment-related activities based in the cottages.

The main differences in the structure of the treatment and corrections staff were as follows: at Federal East treatment and corrections staff were merged into a single department headed by a caseworker and assisted by a corrections officer. The same structure was replicated at the cottage level, the cottage being supervised by a caseworker assisted by a corrections officer. The treatment staff was closely involved in the day-to-day operations of the cottages, and the corrections staff had important responsibilities in carrying out complex and pervasive treatment activities. Both within and without of the cottages, however, the corrections personnel were in a subordinate position to the treatment staff. At Federal West the treatment and corrections staff were separate and distinct. Caseworkers were located within a separate department and provided casework services. Corrections personnel supervised much of the inmates' activities within and without the cottage, and most of the decisions were made by the corrections supervisors and Chief Correctional Supervisor who were responsible for the security and control of the institution. Corrections staff were only marginally involved in treatment programs, and treatment staff had little say in the day-to-day handling of the inmates.

Overall, the program complexity at Federal East created more reciprocal interdependence, which required a more integrated organizational structure, as is reflected by the fact that Federal East had only four major departments as contrasted to Federal West, which had ten. Federal West, utilizing simpler change and control technologies and lacking technologies that required interdepartmental cooperation, did not require as much integration and was able to operate effectively with multiple autonomous departments.

Another very important aspect of staff structure is the number of staff or ratio of inmates to staff in the institution and the allocation of these staff to the different departments. Federal East had a much more favorable inmate-staff ratio than did Federal West. This is due at least in part to the fact that Federal East was a recently opened institution and had not yet reached capacity in terms of the inmate population at the time, although it opened with what was considered an almost complete complement of staff.

Federal East, with a complement of 161 staff and an inmate population of 176, had an inmate-staff ratio of 1.1. On the other hand, Federal West with a complement of 155 staff and an inmate population of approximately 312 had an inmate-staff ratio of 2.0. The inmate-staff ratios by departments reflected the emphasis given different programs at the two institutions. While the ratio was in all cases more favorable at Federal East, the difference was greatest in terms of the inmate-cottage staff ratio (3.7 at Federal East, 10.1 at Federal West), the area in which most of Federal East's treatment activities were located. On the other hand, the ratios were most closely alike for the inmate-teacher ratios (13.5 at Federal East, 14.2 at Federal West), education being the program component receiving the most emphasis at Federal West.

Staff Characteristics. While organizational features such as goals and treatment ideologies constitute major influences affecting the organizational climate of an institution, the staff can also be viewed as inputs to the total configuration. Staff backgrounds will reflect the belief of the executives as to the types of personnel best-suited to work with the inmates, will be indicative of the amenability of the staff to new belief systems, and, in a general way, will indicate the level of resources the institution is willing to commit to pursue its goals. Other factors, of course, enter into the composition of the staff, foremost of which is the availability of certain staff within the immediate environment.

The staff at Federal East tended to be younger, to be slightly less educated, to have less experience with the Bureau of Prisons (and corrections in general), and to include a slightly larger percentage of females than the staff at Federal West. These differences were to a great extent the result of local hiring for a new institution located in what was basically a rural area. The marked differences in the age of staff at the two institutions (median age at Federal East was 37, at Federal West it was 47) was related to the manpower pool available in the immediate area surrounding Federal East, as well as a belief on the part of recruiters that the director of the institution preferred a young staff. The lower education of the Federal East staff (11.8 years of education compared to 12.4 at Federal West) also reflects differences in the general education level of the population around the institution and the population to be found in the area of Federal West. Local hiring also resulted in a staff at Federal East that had much less experience than the staff at Federal West. There was a larger percentage of females at Federal East reflecting an increased openness and acceptance of female staff members, although female staff at both institutions were limited to the business and education departments.

The small differences between the two institutions probably reflected the contingencies of the local manpower pools more than conscious design by the institution administrators or the Bureau of Prisons. While in some respects the younger, less educated, less experienced staff at Federal East presented some problems in terms of working with inmates, these same characteristics probably made it more open to new beliefs about changing inmates, more flexible in terms of trying new techniques, and possibly closer to the inmates in terms of social distance.

Staff Perspectives. We have, in earlier sections of this chapter, reviewed the differences in goals, program technologies, and staff structure that existed between the two institutions. Federal East and Federal West differed in the goals they emphasized, the change technologies seen as appropriate for the pursuit of those goals, and the structuring of staff roles that would be most effective in implementing those technologies. We expect these differences in organizational components to result in differences in staff perspectives regarding the handling of inmates and these differences in perspective, in turn, to contribute to differences in the organizational climates prevailing at the two institutions. In this section we will examine staff perspectives on crime and offenders, on the inmate population with which they worked, and on the best ways for the inmates to get along in the institutions.

We examined the general attitudes of staff toward crime and offenders through the scoring of four attitudinal dimensions obtained through a factor analysis of nineteen questionnaire items. The four dimensions that emerged from the factor analysis can best be described as an offender behavior dimension (e.g., "Inmates who get the most out of their stay keep to themselves"), a treatment dimension (e.g., "Young offenders need a chance to express feelings without punishment"), a societal control dimension (e.g., "The Supreme Court has gone too far in protecting criminals"), and a discipline dimension (e.g., "Young offenders have to be punished to learn correct behavior").

Comparing the mean scores of the staff at Federal East and Federal West, we found fairly substantial differences on three of the four dimensions; on the treatment dimension the staff attitudes were most alike. On the dimensions where differences did exist, the staff at Federal East tended to disagree with items calling for more discipline and crime control and with items that presented offenders as strange or different. Thus, while the staff appeared to be very similar in their attitudes regarding importance of treating youths nonpunitively and with sympathetic understanding, they differed significantly in terms of other attitudes that were congruent and supportive of a treatment orientation in dealing with offenders. These differences resulted from differences in the prevailing organizational ideologies rather than from marked differences in staff backgrounds.

Not only did differences exist in the generalized attitudes of the staffs toward crime and offenders, but there were also marked differences in the attitudes of the staffs regarding the inmates with whom they worked on a daily basis. We found substantial differences in the degree of optimism held by staff regarding the probability that the inmates with which they were working would improve. Almost half of the staff at Federal East felt the majority of the inmates would improve, while less than a third of the staff at Federal West were equally optimistic. On the other end of the scale we found less than a fifth of the Federal East staff believing that the majority of inmates will not improve, while over a third of the Federal West staff took this pessimistic position.

Closely related to the staffs' optimism regarding inmate change potential were the staffs' perceptions of the extent to which the inmates could be trusted. When presented with the statement, "Most young offenders can't be trusted," 31 percent of the staff at Federal East indicated they agreed; 39 percent of the staff at Federal West agreed with this item. While a substantial minority of the staff at both institutions felt there is reason to distrust the inmates, this mistrust appears to vary in intensity and focus at the two institutions. Over 50 percent of the staff at Federal West felt that "all or many of the inmates will run if we don't keep a close watch on them;" only 29 percent of the staff at Federal East felt that this was so.

The staffs' general beliefs toward crime and offenders and their perceptions of the inmates with whom they work will be related to their beliefs regarding the best modes of inmate management. Some staff believe that inmates should be isolated from each other, conform to staff orders, and that all inmates should be treated alike, while others believe that interaction among the inmates should be encouraged, that immediate and strict conformity to staff orders should not always be expected or required, and that there should be differential handling of individual inmates. The underlying dimensions of these contrasting orientations may be identified as *Isolation, Conformity*, and *Universalism*. To measure staff beliefs in these areas, a staff prisonization scale previously developed by Street, Vinter, and Perrow was utilized.[10] This scale consists of three items which formed a Guttman-type scale:

Isolation: "Inmates who get the most out of their stay here keep to themselves and don't get too close to the other inmates."

Conformity: "The best way for an inmate to get along here is to do what he's told and to do it quickly."

Universalism: "All inmates should receive the same discipline for breaking a rule."

Staff who generally agreed that inmates should keep to themselves, do what they are told, and receive the same disciplinary treatment were classified Type I—high prisonization—while those who generally disagreed with these items were classified as Type IV—low prisonization. Intermediate types were those who agreed with some items, disagreed with others. We found that only 5 percent of the Federal East staff had scores in the Type I category, high prisonization, in contrast to 19 percent of the Federal West staff. Conversely, only 21 percent of the Federal West staff scored in the Type IV category, low prisonization, in contrast to 39 percent of the Federal East staff. The Federal West staff, to a much greater extent than the Federal East staff, saw an emphasis on isolation, conformity, and universalism as the appropriate modes of inmate management. In short, they saw a greater need for a restrictive rather than permissive environment.

The Importation Model and Inmate Background Characteristics

In the importation model of prisonization the inmate subculture is seen as a reflection of the values and norms that the inmates bring with them into the institutional setting. In this model the organizational climate becomes of secondary importance; the previous experiences of the inmates is of primary significance. The key to understanding the inmate system then involves knowledge of the backgrounds of the inmates. In those settings where we find inmates with the most negative backgrounds (e.g., lower socioeconomic class, more numerous and more serious offenses) we would expect to find the most prisonized inmate systems; we would expect to find those inmates with such characteristics to be the most "prisonized" inmates within that setting. This contrasts with the prediction derived from the deprivation model that significance of inmate background characteristics will vary from institution to institution depending on their meanings within the prevailing ideology held by the staff.

Personal Characteristics of the Inmates

The majority of the inmates at both institutions were between eighteen and twenty-one years of age. Ninety-three percent of the inmates at Federal East and 90 percent of the inmates at Federal West were within this age bracket. The majority of inmates at both institutions were white, although there were sizeable groups of inmates of other racial backgrounds. Federal West differed from Federal East in that nonwhite inmates made up a slightly larger proportion of the inmate body (30 percent versus 25 percent) and in that Indian inmates constituted the largest nonwhite group (18 percent Indian versus 12 percent black). At Federal East Indians constituted a much smaller percentage of the population (2 percent). The social class backgrounds of the inmates at the two institutions were very similar with approximately one-fourth of the inmates coming from white-collar backgrounds, while approximately one-fifth of the inmates were from homes where no one was in the labor force at the time of their incarceration. Although the vast majority of the inmates were eighteen or older, only a small minority had completed high school (11 percent at Federal East and 15 percent at Federal West). The proportion who had not yet finished the eighth grade was almost twice as large at Federal East (15 percent) than at Federal West (8 percent), although in general the educational backgrounds of the inmates at the two institutions were very similar. The distribution of intelligence scores are even more alike, although percentage-wise there are slightly more inmates in the "superior" category (I.Q. score of 111 or more) at Federal West than at Federal East and slightly fewer in the "below normal" category (I.Q. score of 90 or less). Over half of the inmates at both institutions came from homes where one or both of their natural parents were no longer present, this condition prevailing for 63 percent of Federal West inmates and for 52 percent of the Federal East inmates. In terms of urban-rural residence, the inmates at Federal East were more likely to have come from a rural background; the proportion of inmates coming from counties that were classified as less than 40 percent urban was ten percentage points larger at Federal East than at Federal West (28 percent versus 18 percent), and the percentage coming from counties classified as 80 percent or more urban was ten percentage points smaller at Federal East than at Federal West (46 percent versus 56 percent).

Offense-Related Characteristics of the Inmates

The distribution of commitment offenses of the inmates mirrors the structure of federal statutes: the vast majority of crimes involved offenses against property and were committed on government property, against government agencies, or involved crossing state boundaries. Auto theft was the single largest category at both institutions; at Federal East auto theft accounted for 62 percent of the commitment offenses, while at Federal West it accounted for 47 percent of the commitment offenses. There were proportionately slightly more drug offenses at Federal West than at Federal East; these were mostly drug offenses involving the violation of laws governing the possession, transportation, or sale of marijuana. There were proportionately more "person-oriented" offenses among the commitment offenses at Federal West than at Federal East (12 percent versus 1 percent). The proportion of inmates in the other offense categories and the overall distribution of offenses were very similar. More inmates at Federal West than Federal East were committed to the institution in conjunction with a violation of probation or parole (15 percent versus 6 percent), although the vast majority of commitments at the two institutions did not involve such violations. Proportionately more inmates at Federal West have been involved in numerous (eight or more) offense incidents than at Federal East (17 percent versus 7 percent), although the vast majority of inmates at both institutions had somewhere between one to seven previous encounters with the law. This commitment was the first experience of extended institutionalization for 54 percent of the inmates at Federal East and for 39 percent of the inmates at Federal West. For those cases where the duration of previous institutionalization could be determined, the patterns of previous institutionalization seemed to be very similar, with less than 10 percent (9 percent at Federal West and 6 percent at Federal East) having spent more than a total of twelve months in an institution of any kind. Of those who had previously spent time in an institution, the largest proportion had spent their longest period of institutionalization in public institutions for delinquents. Proportionately more of the Federal East inmates who had been previously institutionalized had spent their longest period of institutionalization in local jails than Federal West inmates, but Federal West inmates who had been previously institutionalized were more likely than their Federal East counterparts to have been in a federal correctional facility prior to this commitment (19 percent versus 3 percent).

Organizationally Assigned Characteristics of the Inmates

We also examined what we have designated "organizationally assigned characteristics" of the inmates at Federal East and Federal West. This label was chosen to emphasize that these characteristics reflected the behavior of the institutions as well as the behavior of the individual inmates.

Half of the inmates at Federal East had been at that institution for between seven and nine months. These inmates with the longest length of stay are the inmates who were transferred to Federal East when the institution opened eight months prior to the time of this study. Fifty-two inmates or approximately 30 percent of the total inmate group at Federal East had spent at least a month at another federal youth center before their transfer. While there were inmates with longer lengths of stay at Federal West, almost two-thirds of the inmate group there had been in the institution nine months or less, and only about one tenth of the inmates had been there longer than fifteen months.

As discussed earlier in this chapter, a rather elaborate treatment typology system was utilized at Federal East. The inmates were fairly well distributed across the five behavior categories used, with slightly more inmates being classified as being BC-4s, subcultural delinquents, and slightly fewer being classified as BC-3s, psychopathic aggressive delinquents.

At Federal East the inmates were almost evenly distributed in the three categories (trainee, apprentice, honor) of the class privilege system. At Federal West almost half (45 percent) of the inmates were classified as requiring "close custody" and were not allowed outside of the main perimeter of the institution.

An attempt had been made at Federal East to handle disciplinary problems on a very individualized basis. There was no routine classification of misconduct incidents into minor and major categories as there was at Federal West. Rather than attempt to classify the misconduct reports found in the files at Federal East, we have reported them all as major misconduct reports on the assumption that the more serious misconduct incidents would be more likely to have been reported and acted on officially. Sixty percent of the Federal East inmates had no misconduct reports. At Federal West 46 percent of the inmates were without major misconduct reports, while 63 percent were without minor misconduct reports. Although it is possible that inmates commit major violations of institutional rules more often than they commit minor violations, these data more likely reflect the differential propensity of staff to officially record major violations and deal with others on an informal basis.

Over two-fifths (44 percent) of the inmates at Federal West had spent some time in the segregation unit. While half of those who had ever been in segregation were only there once, 8 percent of the inmate population had been in four or more times. At Federal East only 17 percent of the population had ever been in the segregation unit. While approximately one-third of the inmates at Federal West had longer lengths of stay than any inmates at Federal East, it is doubtful that this factor alone could account for the differences in the use of the segregation unit. At Federal West the segregation unit was routinely used as a disciplinary measure for many kinds of violations; at Federal East it was used more or less as a last resort and was considered an extraordinary measure.

Summary

We began this chapter with a discussion of the deprivation model of prisonization and the significance of organizational climates within that model. We then went on to describe various aspects of the organizational climates at Federal East and Federal West.

At Federal East we found a new and elaborate physical plant providing facilities for the educational and recreational as well as everyday living requirements of the inmates. At Federal West we found an older, more traditional physical plant with many of the facilities designed for custodial purposes.

A very explicit and detailed statement of goals emphasized treatment and rehabilitation at Federal East. The unpromulgated goals of Federal West centered on education and custody. The staff at both institutions ranked education and training as the most important objectives of the institutions. The staff at Federal East, however, saw treatment and community concerns as the next priority, whereas the staff at Federal West ranked custody and control concerns as their second priority.

The program components at the two institutions also contributed to the maintenance of different organizational climates. At Federal East an explicit rationale provided the basis for classifying inmates according to treatment needs; at Federal West the classification system was based primarily on security needs. At Federal East an "economy of abundance" prevailed; at Federal West we found an "economy of scarcity." At Federal East the emphasis was on utilizing as mild a sanction as possible; at Federal West discipline was more bureaucratized and routinely involved the loss of goodtime credits and time in the segregation unit. At Federal East counseling was considered a focal activity; at Federal West counseling received relatively little emphasis. Differences also existed in the use of inmates to maintain the physical plants of the institutions: at Federal East the inmates spent 1.5 hours in chore assignments; at Federal West most of the inmates spent at least a half-day on institutional maintenance work details.

Differences in the prerequisites and consequences of the program components placed Federal East relatively close to the permissive pole of our permission-restriction continuum and Federal West closer to the restrictive pole of the continuum.

Important differences also existed in staff structure at the two institutions. The most significant of these was the merger of corrections and treatment staffs at Federal East into a single department headed by a caseworker and the involvement of a professionally trained caseworker in the day-to-day operations of the living unit. In contrast, Federal West maintained the traditional separate and autonomous corrections and treatment departments. Important differences in the inmate-staff ratio also existed at the time, the ratio being more favorable at Federal East.

While not great, there were certain differences in the staff backgrounds at the two institutions. The staff at Federal East tended to have slightly less education and experience, to be slightly younger, and included proportionally slightly more females. While the latter factor may be attributable to design, the other differences probably reflect the contingencies of hiring a new staff and of the given manpower pool.

To a greater extent than would be warranted by the differences in staff backgrounds, there existed differences in staff attitudes. The Federal West staff tended to take a harder line toward crime and delinquents in general, was more likely to mistrust the inmates and expect escape attempts, and more often felt that inmate management should stress isolation, conformity, and universalism. These differences were seen as resulting primarily from differences in the prevailing organizational ideologies and in turn resulted in a more restrictive organizational climate at Federal West.

The importation model of prisonization stresses the importance of the backgrounds of the inmates in determining the character of the inmate system. An examination of the personal characteristics of the inmates at the two institutions revealed that the inmates at Federal West tended to be slightly better educated and more often came from urban backgrounds than the inmates at Federal East. The age distributions and the socioeconomic backgrounds of the two groups were very similar. One marked difference between the institutions was the existence of a sizeable Indian minority (18 percent) at Federal West.

While the commitment offenses of the inmates at the two institutions were not markedly different—public order, drug, and auto theft offenses accounted for 75 percent of the commitments at Federal East and for 68 percent of the commitments at Federal West—the inmates at Federal West were slightly more likely to have committed a crime against a person, to have committed more numerous previous offenses, and to have been previously institutionalized.

An examination of the organizationally assigned characteristics of the inmates indicates that the inmates at Federal West were more likely to have received major misconduct reports and to have been in segregation than their counterparts at Federal East. These data are seen as reflecting institutional policy and staff behavior as well as that of the individual inmates.

In summary, Federal East was characterized by a relatively permissive organizational climate in contrast to that which prevailed at Federal West. According to our model we would expect the responses of the inmates to be less prisonized. In terms of personal background characteristics, neither inmate group appeared to be "disadvantaged" in comparison to the other, and there is little basis for predicting that one would be more "prisonized" than the other on the basis of their background characteristics. The offense backgrounds of the inmates at Federal East tended to be less serious than the inmates at Federal West. This also would lead us to predict that the responses of the inmates at Federal East would be less prisonized. In the next chapter we attempt to answer the two questions raised by these predictions: Do differences exist in the extent of prisonization of the inmate groups at the two institutions? Do organizational climates or inmate background differences influence prisonization to a greater extent?

Notes

1. Robert D. Vinter and Rosemary C. Sarri, *Federal Correctional Programs for Young Offenders: A Comparative Study* (Washington, D.C.: U.S. Department of Justice, 1974).

2. Bernard Berk, "Informal Social Organization and Leadership among Inmates in Treatment and Custodial Prisons: A Comparative Study" (Ph.D. dissertation, University of Michigan, 1961); Oscar Grusky, "Treatment Goals and Organizational Behavior: A Study of an Experimental Prison Camp" (Ph.D. dissertation, University of Michigan, 1957); Rosemary Sarri, "Organizational Patterns and Client Perspectives in Juvenile Correctional Institutions: A Comparative Study" (Ph.D. dissertation, University of Michigan, 1962); David Street, Robert Vinter, and Charles Perrow, *Organization for Treatment* (New York: The Free Press, 1966); and Mayer Zald, "Multiple Goals and Staff Structure: A Comparative Study of Correctional Institutions for Juvenile Delinquents" (Ph.D. dissertation, University of Michigan, 1960).

3. Given the fact that we are dealing with a two-case comparative study it is unnecessary and unfeasible to attempt to quantify the permissiveness-restrictiveness dimension of the organizational climates, and we will only attempt to demonstrate that Federal East is indeed more permissive than Federal West. For a methodological approach to classifying the organizational climates of a larger number of organizations, see Ronald Akers, Norman Hayner, and Werner Gruninger, "Homosexual and Drug Behavior in Prison: A Test of the Functional and Importation Models of the Inmate System," *Social Problems* 21 (1974): 410-422.

4. Bureau of Prisons, *Differential Treatment . . . a way to begin* (Washington D.C.: U.S. Department of Justice), pp. IX-X.

5. Edward Gross, "Universities as Organizations: A Research Approach," *American Sociological Review* 33 (1968): 518-544.

6. For a more comprehensive discussion of these goals and the changes in goals at Federal East over time, see Donald T. Dickson, "Environments, Goals and Technology: An Analysis of Organizational Change in a New Juvenile Correctional Institution" (Ph.D. dissertation, University of Michigan, 1973).

7. Bureau of Prisons, *Differential Treatment*, pp. 6-7.

8. Ibid., p. 8.

9. Ibid., p. 33.

10. Street, Vinter, and Perrow, *Organization for Treatment*, pp. 176-177.

4

Prisonization and Integration: Empirical Findings

In this chapter we will examine more closely, in the light of the empirical findings, three of the five sets of hypotheses presented earlier in Chapter 2: Major Variables Affecting the Alternate Society, Integration within the Alternate Society, and Integration and Inmate Adaptations.

Methodological Notes

The two organizational settings that are the subjects of this research were not selected on the basis of random sampling but rather were selected on the basis of other criteria unrelated to the immediate concerns of this analysis. Consequently no claims are made that these settings are "random samples." Furthermore, the questionnaire on which most of the analysis is based was administered, with only minor exceptions, to the entire inmate populations at the two institutions, and there was no sampling within the two settings. Given these circumstances and the ongoing debate regarding the value of tests of statistical significance in circumstances that depart even less from the ideal assumptions required for their use, it was decided that tests of significance would not be utilized in analyzing the data.[1] Furthermore, it was decided that the limitations of the level of measurement of the data would be strictly observed in the choice of any measures of association. The data essentially consist of questionnaire and file information constituting nominal and ordinal scale variables gathered at two organizational settings, which can be rank-ordered on a permissiveness-restrictiveness dimension. The statistical measures of association selected as most appropriate for the analysis task were gamma, for measuring the relationship between two ordinal level variables with two or more categories; Yule's Q, a special case of gamma appropriate for use with either two dichotomous ordinal variables or with two dichotomous nominal scale variables; and Goodman and Kruskal's tau for measuring the relationship between two nominal scale variables with more than two categories.[2] In the following discussion of the empirical findings we will be interested in whether or not an association exists between two variables, in the sign or direction of that association, and in the strength of the association. Rather than setting arbitrary levels for the acceptance or rejection of our hypotheses, we will content ourselves with noting whether or not the data support or contradict these hypotheses and the strength of the supportive or contrary evidence.

For the sake of consistency the following conventions will be used throughout the textual discussion to describe the strength of the statistical associations measured by gamma (γ), Yule's Q, and Goodman and Kruskal's tau (τ):

.00	No association
.01 to .09	A negligible association
.10 to .19	A low association
.20 to .39	A moderate association
.40 to .59	A substantial association
.60 or higher	A very strong association

Indices have been utilized to operationalize a number of key concepts in this chapter, and the construction of these indices will be discussed as these concepts are introduced.

Major Variables Affecting the Alternate Society

In Chapter 2 we presented a number of hypotheses regarding the relationships we would expect to find between organizational climates and the nonprisonized and prisonized adaptations of the inmates. We have already discussed the concept of organizational climates and the empirical indicators we used in designating Federal East a permissive organizational climate and Federal West a restrictive organizational climate. We have yet to discuss what is meant by nonprisonized and prisonized adaptations and specifically how these concepts were operationalized for this study.

Prisonization was originally defined by Clemmer as "*the taking on in greater or less degree of the folkways, mores, customs, and general culture of the penitentiary.*"[3] The culture of the penitentiary was distinguished most clearly from the general culture of outside society by its emphasis on opposition to authority figures, on solidarity among inmates, on doing one's own "time" as easily as possible, and on not ever doing anything that is likely to cause another inmate to do longer or harder "time." To measure the extent to which inmates were prisonized, Stanton Wheeler in his now classic study of the Washington State Reformatory devised a series of prison vignettes to which both staff and inmates were asked to respond.[4] Staff responses to the vignettes were accepted as representing societal or prosocial role expectations for the inmates. Those inmate responses that conformed with the expectations of the majority of staff were seen as conforming or nonprisonized responses; those inmate responses that differed from the expectations of the majority of the staff were seen as nonconforming or prisonized responses. These responses were then combined into a five-item conformity index on which the inmates were scored low (conforming on none or one item), medium (conforming on two or three items), and high (conforming on four or all five items).

A modified form of the Wheeler vignettes and conformity index was used at Federal East and Federal West. The staff and inmates were asked to indicate what they thought the inmate in the vignette should do or whether they approved of what he had done and to indicate how they thought the other inmates would feel about the situation. The responses to this second set of questions were compared with the responses to the first set of questions to measure the extent of pluralistic ignorance (i.e., the difference between the attitudes *actually* held by individuals and what were believed to be the attitudes held by the same group of individuals). Briefly, the vignettes used and the prosocial or conforming responses to each were as follows:

1. Smith and Henry are planning an escape. They threaten Jones with a beating unless he steals a crowbar for them from the tool shop where he works. He thinks they mean business. While he is trying to smuggle the crowbar into the unit, he is caught by an officer and is charged with planning to escape. If he doesn't describe the whole situation, he may have his sentence extended up to a year. He can avoid it by blaming Smith and Henry.

   What should Jones do?

   Conforming response: He should clear himself by telling about the escape plans of Smith and Henry.

2. Owens is assigned to a work detail. Some other guys criticize him because he works as hard as he can and does more work than anyone else on the detail.

   How do you personally feel about Owen's action?

   Conforming responses: Strongly Approve, Approve.

3. Smith and Long are very good friends. Smith has a five-dollar bill that was smuggled into the institution by a visitor. Smith tells Long he thinks the officers are suspicious and asks Long to hide the money for him for a few days. Long takes the money and hides it.

   How do you personally feel about Long's hiding the money?

   Conforming responses: Disapprove, Strongly Disapprove.

4. Martin goes before a committee that makes job assignments. He is given a choice between two jobs. One job would call for hard work, but it would give Martin training that might be useful to him on the outside.

The other job would allow Martin to do easier time in the institution. But it provides no training for a job on the outside. Martin decided to take the easier job.

How do you personally feel about Martin's deciding to take the easier job?

Conforming responses: Disapprove, Strongly Disapprove.

5. A guy, without thinking, commits a minor rule infraction. He is given a "write-up" by a correctional officer who saw the violation. Later three other guys are talking to each other about it. Two of them criticize the officer. The third guy, Sykes, defends the officer saying the officer was only doing his duty.

How do you personally feel about Sykes' defending the officer?

Conforming responses: Strongly Approve, Approve.

The staffs at both Federal East and Federal West were virtually unanimous in their choice of the appropriate course of action in each situation, the inmates considerably less so. The responses of the inmates to these vignettes constitute a test of our first set of hypotheses.

Organizational Climates and Inmate Adaptations

Hypothesis 1a *Inmate groups in permissive organizational climates will be characterized by nonprisonized adaptations; inmate groups in restrictive organizational climates will be characterized by prisonized adaptations.*

According to Hypothesis 1a we would expect the inmates at Federal East to give conforming or prosocial responses more often than the inmates at Federal West. The data indicated that this was indeed the case. For all situations except one the inmates at Federal East were more likely than the Federal West inmates to respond in terms of staff-approved norms of conduct. The only situation for which the Federal West inmates were more likely to select the prosocial or conforming responses involved working hard on a work detail, and here the difference was one of only a few percentage points. As previously discussed, work details had quite different meanings at the two institutions. At Federal West 20 percent of the inmates worked full-time on institutional work details and another 50 percent worked half-time on such details, while at Federal East the inmates spent less than two hours a day on institutional work details. At Federal West the work details often provided valuable vocational training and were the main source through which inmates could receive Meritorious Service Award (MSA) payments. At Federal East the work details more often were minor chores, and the inmates had many other opportunities to earn funds or points in other components of the token economy system. Working as hard as one could had both greater short-run and long-run payoffs at Federal West, and it is not surprising that slightly more of the Federal West inmates chose the prosocial or conforming responses for this situation.

Summing the number of conforming responses over all five situations we obtain the distribution presented in Table 4-1. Viewing our two organizational sites as representing different degrees of permissiveness-restrictiveness, we find a moderately strong negative association between conformity and restrictiveness as indicated by the gamma of —.30. This finding lends support to Hypothesis 1a and the deprivation model of prisonization. It does not, however, allow us to examine the utility of the alternate explanation, the importation model. Hypotheses 1b, 1c, and 1d deal with the importation model and its relative utility vis-a-vis the deprivation model. We will examine these below.

Background Characteristics and Inmate Adaptations

Hypothesis 1b *Inmates with relatively prosocial backgrounds will manifest nonprisonized adaptations to the institution experience; inmates with relatively antisocial backgrounds will manifest prisonized adaptations to the institutional experience.*

To test this hypothesis we examined the conformity index scores of the inmates at Federal East and Federal West, controlling for the various personal, offense, and organizational characteristics discussed in the previous chapter.

Table 4-1
Inmate Conformity Index Scores
(percentages)

	Federal East	Federal West
Low conformity (0 or 1 conforming responses)	12	18
Medium conformity (2 or 3 conforming responses)	41	52
High conformity (4 or 5 conforming responses)	47	30
	(157)	(276)
	$\gamma = -.30$	

Personal Characteristics. We examined the conformity index scores of the Federal East and Federal West inmates controlling for the personal background characteristics of age, race, social class, education, intelligence, family composition, and residence. Whatever associations there were between the personal characteristics of the inmates and their conformity index scores lent little support to the importation model of prisonization; on the contrary, these findings support the deprivation model to a greater extent. There was virtually no relationship at either institution between the responses of the inmates and their age, race, education, or previous residence. There were but low associations between conformity responses and social class and intelligence at both institutions and family composition at Federal West. The only association of even moderate strength ($\gamma = -.28$) was that between conformity and family composition at Federal East: those inmates coming from homes where both natural parents were present were less likely to give conforming responses than those inmates coming from homes where one or both of their natural parents were no longer in the home.

The negative associations between the conformity scores and social class, education, intelligence, and family composition at Federal West were as one would predict on the basis of the importation model of prisonization. However, the associations between conformity and three of these variables (social class, education, and family composition) were positive at Federal East. It appears, therefore, that the same background characteristics took on different meanings and led to different outcomes in different institutional settings, a conclusion consistent with the tenets of the deprivation model of prisonization. Furthermore, while the relationships were not very strong, it appears that those inmates at Federal East who were more poorly educated, came from lower-class homes, and came from homes where at least one natural parent was absent were more likely to conform to staff-endorsed norms for behavior within the institution. It seems that inmates from relatively deprived backgrounds were reacting in a more favorable manner to the relatively permissive and comfortable organizational climate than were the inmates coming from better backgrounds, a finding that also is consistent with the deprivation model of prisonization.

Offense-Related Characteristics. The offense-related characteristics we used as controls included type of commitment offense, probation-parole violation status, number of previous offense incidents, length of previous institutionalization, and type of longest previous institutionalization.

We rank ordered the commitment offenses of the inmates in the following manner: Public Order (delinquency, Selective Service, drug offenses), Auto Theft, Other Theft, and Person-Oriented (robbery, assault).

Looking at the relationships between conformity responses and offense-related characteristics of the inmates we found a low positive relationship between conformity scores and severity of the offense for which the inmate was committed at Federal East ($\gamma = +.19$) and a negligible negative association at Federal West ($-.09$). Once again, the strength of the relationships was not very great, and the signs of the association were opposite. While the relationship between conformity and whether or not the inmate was a probation or parole violator was a substantial positive one at Federal East ($\gamma = +.44$), the very small proportion of inmates who were probation or parole violators made it necessary for us to discount this measure of association. The association between conformity and this variable at Federal West was a negligible negative one ($\gamma = -.02$).

The number of previous offense incidents in which an inmate had been involved has generally been accepted as a measure of the concept, "antisocial background." We will examine this assumption more closely later in this chapter; for the present, we note that the relationship between this variable and the conformity responses was negative and of moderate strength at both institutions, a gamma of $-.37$ at Federal East and of $-.26$ at Federal West. This relationship is consistent with the importation model of prisonization as we have explicated it, and it does not appear to have been affected by the organizational setting. The magnitude of the association was similar to that found between conformity and organizational setting ($\gamma = -.30$) found earlier. This raises the question of the relative utility of the deprivation and importation models, a question we will address in our discussion of hypotheses 1c and 1d.

The sign of the low association ($\gamma = -.16$) between conformity and length of previous institutionalization at Federal East and the sign of the negligible association ($\gamma = -.08$) between these variables at Federal West are both negative; this finding is consistent with the finding of a negative relationship between conformity and number of previous offense incidents and is also supportive of the hypothesis derived from the importation model. The relationship between the type of longest institutionalization and the conformity responses are similar at both institutions, gamma equaling $+.19$ at Federal East and $+.22$ at Federal West, indicating that those inmates whose longest previous institutionalization was in a correctional facility other than an institution for juveniles are more likely to give prosocial responses. Those inmates whose longest previous period of institutionalization was in an institution for juveniles were more likely to give prisonized responses. This finding seems to contradict the relationship one might expect between conformity orientations and previous institutionalization, but taking into consideration the fact that commitment to juvenile facilities tends to be more open-ended and therefore for longer periods of time and that young offenders would be more likely to remain on the fringes of the inmate subculture in an adult facility, it is consistent with the more general model of the alternate society we have presented.

Organizationally Assigned Characteristics. Length of stay, treatment classification, and career level at Federal East, custody status and minor misconduct reports at Federal West, number of major misconduct reports, and the number of times the inmate was in segregation were the organizationally assigned characteristics we used as controls in analyzing the conformity scores of the inmates.

Consideration of the relationships that existed between the conformity index scores and organizationally assigned characteristics produced a number of relationships worthy of note. A moderate negative relationship between conformity and length of stay ($\gamma = -.23$ at Federal East, $\gamma = -.27$ at Federal West) replicated a relationship found numerous times in previous studies: the longer the length of stay the more likely the inmates were to give nonconforming or prisonized responses, a finding consistent with the explanation offered by the deprivation model of prisonization. On the other hand, the program variables at Federal East, treatment classification and career level, had virtually no association with the conformity scores of the inmates. At Federal West there was a low association ($\gamma = +.16$) between custody and conformity, with those inmates classified as needing close supervision slightly more likely to give conforming responses than those classified as needing minimum supervision. We found moderate to substantial negative associations at both institutions between conformity responses and the number of misconduct reports ($\gamma = -.29$ at Federal East, $\gamma = -.31$ at Federal West) and the number of times the inmates had been in the segregation units ($\gamma = -.42$ at Federal East, $\gamma = -.26$ at Federal West). These relationships may be seen as validating the conformity index measure, the misconduct reports and the segregation placements representing behavioral correlates of the nonconforming or prisonized orientations of the inmates.

While most of the associations found above were either very weak, in a direction other than that hypothesized, or different at the two organizational sites, we found some support for Hypothesis 1b and the importation model of prisonization. Using the number of previous offense incidents in which an inmate was involved as a measure of "antisocial background," we found that inmates from relatively antisocial backgrounds indeed were more likely to give nonconforming or prisonized responses than inmates from relatively prosocial backgrounds. Thus far we have found support for both the deprivation model of prisonization as stated in Hypothesis 1a and for the importation model of prisonization as stated in Hypothesis 1b. In Hypothesis 1c we proceed to examine the outcomes of both extreme and intermediate combinations of permissive and restrictive organizational climates and prosocial and antisocial inmate backgrounds.

Organizational Climates and Inmate Background
Characteristics: Interactive Effects

Hypothesis 1c *The organizational climate of the institution and the*
preinstitutional orientations of the inmates will interact with additive effects
resulting in extreme nonprisonized or prisonized adaptations or with cancel-
ing effects resulting in adaptations of an intermediate variety.

This hypothesis states that in those situations where we find prosocial
inmates in a permissive organizational climate they will be the least prisonized; where we find antisocial inmates in a restrictive environment, they will
be the most prisonized; and where we find prosocial inmates in a restrictive
organizational climate or antisocial inmates in a permissive organizational
climate, they will be prisonized to an intermediate degree. Table 4-2
presents the conformity index scores for inmates of prosocial and antisocial
backgrounds in the two organizational settings.

The responses of the inmates were indeed ordered as predicted: the prosocial inmates at Federal East were the most conforming or least prisonized,
while the responses of the antisocial inmates at Federal West were the least
conforming or most prisonized. The responses of the antisocial inmates at
Federal East and the prosocial inmates at Federal West fell between the two
extreme categories. What also becomes apparent in Table 4-2 is that, while
the responses of the antisocial inmates at Federal East fell between the two
extreme response categories, their responses approximate the responses of

Table 4-2
Conformity Index Scores of Prosocial and Antisocial Inmates in Permissive and
Restrictive Organizational Climates

(percentages)

Conformity Index Scores	Permissive Climate (Federal East)		Restrictive Climate (Federal West)	
	Prosocial (0-3 previous offense incidents)	*Antisocial (4 or more previous offense incidents)*	*Prosocial (0-3 previous offense incidents)*	*Antisocial (4 or more previous offense incidents)*
Low	4	22	13	22
Medium	38	48	48	54
High	58	30	39	24
	(95)	(60)	(122)	(153)
		$\gamma = -.33$		

the antisocial inmates at Federal West. In other words, it appears that the number of previous offense incidents the inmate was involved in has a greater association with his responses than the organizational climate in which he is located. This issue was raised directly in Hypothesis 1d, which we will discuss more fully below.

Organizational Climates and Inmate
Background Characteristics: Primary
and Secondary Influences

Hypothesis 1d *The organizational climate within which the inmates are located will be of primary importance in influencing the adaptations of the inmates; the preinstitutional orientations of the inmates constitute an important, although secondary influence on the adaptations of the inmates.*

The findings presented in Table 4-2 appear to contradict this hypothesis. Table 4-3 presents the same data in a slightly different format, allowing us to estimate the impact of the organizational climate variable when inmate backgrounds are controlled.

In Table 4-3 we see that there was a moderate relationship between organizational climate and the conformity response of inmates who had been involved in three or less recorded offense incidents prior to being incarcerated, gamma equaling $-.39$ for those with no previous offense incidents and $-.36$ for those who were involved in one to three previous offense incidents. However, for those who had been involved in four or more previous offense incidents there was only a negligible association between

Table 4-3

Inmate Conformity Scores Controlled by Number of Previous Offense Incidents *(percentages)*

| | Number of Previous Offense Incidents | | | | | |
| | None | | 1-3 | | 4+ | |
Conformity Index Scores	Federal East	Federal West	Federal East	Federal West	Federal East	Federal West
Low	10	4	3	15	22	22
Medium	37	73	38	42	48	54
High	53	23	59	43	30	24
	(19)	(22)	(76)	(100)	(60)	(153)
	$\gamma = -.39$		$\gamma = -.36$		$\gamma = -.08$	

organizational setting and conformity responses. Contrary to our hypothesis stated above, the preinstitutional orientations of the inmates as measured by involvement in previous law violations were of primary importance in influencing the adaptations of the inmates. Organizational climate constituted an important, but secondary, influence. Some care must be taken in interpreting this relationship, however. Offense records probably serve as much as indicators of the behavior of the agents of social control as they do the criminal behavior of the offender. The number of previous offenses in an inmate's record is probably a more valid indicator of the amount of his experience with the justice system than his number of law-violating acts. We therefore see the inmate's offense record as an indicator of his experience as an offender in the criminal justice system. The findings reported in Table 4-2 and 4-3 may then be interpreted as meaning that those inmates who have had the most prior experience in the criminal justice system are the most prisonized, regardless of the organizational climate in which they are found. Further, it is possible that their negative orientations may be explainable in terms of the deprivation model at an earlier point in their careers. However, if by imported variables we mean those which the inmate brings with him into the current situation, whatever their origin, we must conclude that while the deprivation and importation models both help us understand prisonization, the importation model appears to offer slightly more predictive power in these settings.

Integration Within the Alternate Society

To what extent does the inmate become involved in interpersonal relationships with other inmates in the institution? To what extent does such involvement vary from organizational setting to organizational setting? What other factors are related to involvement with others within the institutional setting? To what extent does involvement with others within the institution serve as a substitute for contacts with family and friends outside the institution? It is to these questions that our second set of hypotheses is addressed.

Organizational Climates and Integration

Hypothesis 2a *Inmates located in institutions characterized by permissive organizational climates will have more highly developed patterns of integration and primary relations than will inmates in institutions characterized by restrictive organizational climates.*

Integration or involvement in primary relationships can be operationalized a number of different ways. Here we will be looking at several different measures of involvement with others and then combining these to create a composite measure of integration. Specifically, we will be examining the intensiveness of association, extensiveness of friendships, and evaluation of acquaintances reported by the inmates at Federal East and Federal West. Table 4-4 presents our operational measures and findings for these three dimensions of integration within the alternate society.

Intensiveness of Association. We found a low positive association ($\gamma = +.15$) between intensiveness of association and a restrictive organizational setting, with the inmates at Federal West reporting that they more often spent their free time in the company of others. There were proportionately fewer inmates in the low category and more in the high category at Federal West than at Federal East. This finding appears to contradict our hypothesis. It deals, however, with only one aspect of integration or involvement in interpersonal relationships, and this aspect, spending time in the presence of others, is one that is particularly sensitive to the demands of institutional scheduling and the parameters set by the physical structure of the institution itself. As was pointed out in Chapter 3, the less regimented schedule and the physical setting of Federal East were more conducive to privacy than the schedule and physical environment at Federal West. The regimentation of the schedule and the housing of most inmates in dormitory settings probably accounts for the greater intensiveness of association found at Federal West.

Extensiveness of Friendships. Another aspect of integration is that of the type of relationship that existed among the inmates; while association may be an important precondition, friendship goes beyond mere association. Examining the inmates' responses regarding the number of friendships they had formed in the institutions, we found only a negligible negative ($\gamma = -.06$) association between extensiveness of friendships and a restrictive organizational climate. The inmates at Federal East were only slightly more likely than the inmates at Federal West to report having formed many friendships within the institution.

Evaluation of Acquaintances. The inmates at the two institutions differed more substantially in terms of their evaluations of their institutional acquaintances. While only about a tenth of the inmates at either institution responded that they would like to see most or almost all of the inmates they have met after they get out, almost three-fourths (72 percent) of the Federal

Table 4-4
Patterns of Integration within the Alternate Society
(percentages)

	Federal East	Federal West
Intensiveness of Association[a]		
Low	24	19
Medium	55	54
High	21	27
	(175)	(304)
	$\gamma = +.15$	
Extensiveness of Friendship[b]		
Low	20	18
Medium	53	60
High	27	22
	(176)	(311)
	$\gamma = -.06$	
Evaluation of Acquaintances[c]		
Low	54	72
Medium	33	18
High	13	10
	(175)	(311)
	$\gamma = -.32$	

[a]Think back over the past month in the institution. How would you say you have spent most of your free time?

Low = Mostly by myself.
Medium = With one or two guys or with several different guys but not in any one group.
High = Mostly with a group of guys who are together a lot.

[b]Have you developed any strong friendships with other guys since you have been in the institution?

Low = No.
Medium = Yes, 1 or 2 or yes, some: 3-5.
High = Yes, many: more than 5.

[c]How many of the guys you have met here would you like to see after you get out?

Low = None or a few.
Medium = Some.
High = Most or almost all.

West inmates reported that they would like to see none or a few of the inmates in contrast to slightly more than half (54 percent) of the Federal East inmates who gave this negative response. Consequently we found a moderately strong negative association ($\gamma = -.32$) between the inmates' evaluations of their acquaintances and a restrictive organizational climate.

Composite Measure of Integration. While the intensiveness of association among inmates was greater at Federal West, the extensiveness of friendships among inmates was slightly greater at Federal East, and the inmates' evaluation of their acquaintances were substantially more positive at Federal East. Which of the above three measures, then, constitutes our best measure of integration or involvement in interpersonal relationships? None of them and all of them. They each measure some aspect of integration or involvement with other inmates. A preliminary factor analysis of these and thirty-five additional items indicated that the responses to these three items—intensiveness of association, extensiveness of friendships, and evaluation of acquaintances—all correlated highly with a factor which might best be termed an "integration factor." Therefore, to adequately measure this integration factor an index was constructed utilizing these three measures. Any inmate who scored high on two out of three of the items and at least medium on the third was recorded as scoring high on the integration index; any inmate who scored low on two of the three items and medium on the third was recorded as scoring low on the integration index; all other inmates were recorded as scoring medium on the integration index. Those who did not answer one or more items were excluded from the index. Table 4-5 presents the integration index scores of the Federal East and Federal West inmates. Using our integration index score as a measure of integration we find a low negative association ($\gamma = -.18$) between integration and a restrictive organizational setting. While the relationship was not very strong, it was as predicted in Hypothesis 2a.

Table 4-5
Inmate Integration Index Scores
(percentages)

Integration Index	Federal East	Federal West
Low	45	55
Medium	26	22
High	29	23
	(174)	(302)
	$\gamma = -.18$	

Contact with Staff and Other Inmates

Hypothesis 2b *Voluntary interaction among inmates will vary directly with the amount of interaction between staff and inmates.*

Unfortunately our data did not include items that would allow us to measure directly "voluntary interaction among inmates" and the "amount of interaction between staff and inmates." We did, however, find at least indirect support for this hypothesis with an item relating to the accessibility of staff at the two institutions. We asked the inmates at both Federal East and Federal West "How often are staff here friendly and easy to approach?" The inmates at Federal East were much more likely to respond "Almost always" or "Often" than the inmates at Federal West (69 percent versus 45 percent), indicating a substantial negative association between the accessibility of staff and a restrictive organizational climate. We have already discussed the negative relationship between integration and a restrictive organizational climate. It appears, therefore, that both integration and accessibility to staff are related to organizational climate. The question remains, however, as to whether or not integration and accessibility are directly related to each other at Federal East and Federal West. Table 4-6 presents data regarding the relationships between these two variables.

At Federal East there was a low positive ($\gamma = +.17$) relationship

Table 4-6
Inmate Integration Index Scores Controlled by Accessibility of Staff
(percentages)

Integration Index	Accessibility of Staff		
	Low	*Medium*	*High*
Federal East			
Low	50	23	26
Medium	43	67	59
High	7	10	15
	(14)	(39)	(121)
		$\gamma = +.17$	
Federal West			
Low	19	21	27
Medium	68	65	64
High	13	14	9
	(62)	(99)	(135)
		$\gamma = -.14$	

between the accessibility of the staff as reported by the inmates and the inmates' integration index scores. Those inmates who reported that staff were accessible were more likely to have higher integration index scores than those inmates who reported that the staff were not accessible. At Federal West the opposite was true: there was a low negative ($\gamma = -.14$) association between accessibility of staff and integration. There the inmates who reported that staff were accessible were more likely to have lower integration index scores. Integration and accessibility of staff appear to be related, but the nature of that relationship depends on the organizational setting. We have found partial support for Hypothesis 2b; at the same time we have established the necessity of qualifying it to take account of the impact of organizational climate.

Phase of Institutional Career and Integration

Hypothesis 2c *Integration is related to the phase of the inmate's institutional career, being low at the beginning of confinement, increasing toward the middle, and decreasing toward release.*

"Phase of institutional career" has in the past been operationalized through the subject reports of the respondents[5] or through the use of panel study procedures.[6] Neither of these methods were employed in obtaining the data we are utilizing, and the best approximation we can make in examining this hypothesis is a cross-sectional analysis of integration scores controlled by total length of stay. It should be emphasized, however, that such a cross-sectional analysis is not an adequate substitution for a measure of career phase as it has been defined previously in the literature. Table 4-7 presents the integration index scores of the Federal East and Federal West inmates, controlled by their total lengths of stay. The integration index scores at neither institution show evidence of the inverted U-shaped pattern predicted by Hypothesis 2c. There is not a strong association between the integration scores and length of stay at either of the institutions, and the signs of the associations that do exist are opposite, there being a low negative association at Federal East and a negligible positive association at Federal West. At Federal East those inmates who have recently entered the institution have the highest percentage in the high integration category and the lowest in the low category of the subgroups. At Federal West just the opposite is the case. Those who have just entered have one of the lowest percentages in the high integration category and the highest percentages in the low category. This is very probably a result of the ways in which the inmates are inducted into the two institutions. At Federal East all incoming inmates are placed into an A and O (Admission and Orientation) cottage where they stay with other

Table 4-7
Inmate Integration Index Scores Controlled by Total Length of Stay
(percentages)

Integration Index	Total Length of Stay (months)				
	1-3	*4-6*	*7-9*	*10-12*	*13 or More*
Federal East					
Low	32	42	49	50	100
Medium	25	38	20	17	
High	43	20	31	33	
	(28)	(56)	(70)	(18)	(1)
			$\gamma = -.11$		
Federal West					
Low	62	53	52	59	53
Medium	20	24	24	26	18
High	18	23	24	15	29
	(74)	(70)	(59)	(27)	(72)
			$\gamma = +.09$		

newcomers who share the same problems of adjustment. At Federal West the inmates are immediately placed in the general population. At Federal East the admission procedure has the effect of facilitating friendships at the beginning, and later the treatment program has the effect of gradually wooing the inmates away from their original associates, resulting in a low negative relationship between integration and length of stay. At Federal West just the opposite occurs. The process of placing new inmates in different living units on a rotation basis does not facilitate immediate integration, and only gradually over time do inmates become increasingly integrated. It therefore appears that at institutions such as these there is little relationship between integration and length of stay and that the types of relationships that do exist are the result of the admission practices of the institutions.

Heterogeneity of the Inmate Group and Integration

Hypothesis 2d *Integration of the inmate group will vary inversely with the heterogeneity of the inmate group.*

Adequate examination of this hypothesis would require numerous populations; here we have but two inmate populations. We can note, however, that our findings are consistent with Hypothesis 2d. One area in which heterogeneity has been found to be especially relevant was that of racial composition. As we discussed in Chapter 3, Federal West had a more racially heterogeneous population, with sizeable minorities of Indians (18 percent) and blacks (12 percent), as well as a number of inmates of Spanish-American descent. At Federal East the population was predominantly white (75 percent); the only other racial group present in significant numbers was that of blacks, who constituted 23 percent of the population. As reported in our discussion of Table 4-5, the integration index scores of the inmates at Federal East were higher than those at Federal West. Thus, while we have only limited data with which to examine this point, the findings are consistent with Hypothesis 2d.

Previous Institutionalization and Integration

Hypothesis 2e *Integration among inmates is inversely related to the amount of correctional confinement they have experienced.*

In our discussion of Hypothesis 2c we reviewed the relationship between the inmate's integration score and length of stay. Hypothesis 2e deals with the relationship between the inmate's previous experience of institutionalization and his current integration within the alternate society. We examined the integration index scores of the Federal East and Federal West inmates controlling for whether they had no previous institutionalization, one to six months of previous institutionalization, or seven or more months of previous institutionalization. While our measure of previous institutionalization included stays in both correctional and noncorrectional facilities, the vast majority of the inmates who had been previously institutionalized had been incarcerated in correctional facilities. There were only negligible associations between length of previous institutionalization and integration at the two institutions ($\gamma = -.09$ at Federal East, $\gamma = +.08$ at Federal West). The signs of the relationships were opposite; no particular pattern appeared in the responses at either setting. It may be that the institutional histories of our inmates were too short to have the impact on integration that Glaser had found previously in examining the friendship and association patterns of older inmates with more extensive histories of institutionalization.[7] Our data, however, offered no support for this hypothesis.

Age and Integration among Inmates

Hypothesis 2f *Integration among inmates is inversely related to the age of the inmates.*

According to the above hypothesis, younger inmates should have had higher integration scores than older inmates. An examination of the inmates' integration index scores controlled by the ages of the inmates (17 or younger, 18, 19, 20, 21 or older) indicated that there was a slight tendency for this to be true at Federal West, but not at Federal East where we found no relationship whatsoever (γ = .00) between age and integration. At Federal West we found a low negative association (γ = $-.17$) between integration and age, congruent with Hypothesis 2f. The total age range at either institution was no greater than eight years. Given such a narrow range it is somewhat surprising to find even the low association we found at Federal West. In spite of the narrow range of values of our independent variable, we have found at least partial support for the hypothesis positing an inverse relationship between age and integration.

Extrainstitutional Ties and Integration

Hypothesis 2g *Integration among the inmates is inversely related to the intensity and extensiveness of extrainstitutional ties maintained by the inmates.*

Hypothesis 2g assumes a zero-sum model of extrainstitutional ties and associations within the institution: the stronger the inmate's ties to the outside world, the weaker his ties to the inmate society, and vice-versa. The data in Table 4-8 suggest, however, that a nonzero-sum model may be more appropriate for this aspect of the inmate's social life. At Federal East we find a moderate positive association (γ = $+.26$) between the frequency of outside contacts and integration; at Federal West we find a low positive association (γ = $+.16$) for the same two variables. These relationships are the opposite of the negative association predicted in Hypothesis 2g. Rather than intra- and extrainstitutional ties being interchangeable, or one serving as a substitute for the other, it appears that the characteristics or conditions that promote one also promote the other. Those inmates who maintain frequent contacts with others outside the institution also tend to be those who are most integrated within the inmate society.

To better understand this phenomenon we examined the relationships that existed between the various component parts of our two indices, the integration index and the outside contacts index. The strongest relationship found among these component items was between the number of contacts with parents and the number of friendships the inmate had made within the institution. We found a moderate positive association at both institutions (γ = $+.38$ at Federal East, γ = $+.35$ at Federal West) between frequency of contact with parents and the inmate's number of friends in the institution. From this distance we can only speculate as to what the underlying dynamics are. One very plausible explanation is that what we are seeing here

Table 4-8
Inmate Integration Index Scores Controlled by Outside Contacts Index Scores
(percentages)

Integration	Outside Contacts Index[a]		
Index	*Low*	*Medium*	*High*
Federal East			
Low	58	50	36
Medium	21	26	28
High	21	24	36
	(29)	(58)	(86)
		$\gamma = +.26$	
Federal West			
Low	56	62	49
Medium	26	22	19
High	18	16	32
	(68)	(116)	(118)
		$\gamma = +.16$	

[a]"About how often do you get in touch with someone outside the institution through either a visit, phone call, or letter: parents, wife, brother or sister, girl friend, buddies?" Inmates who responded "Several times a week" to any of the above categories were scored High; those who responded "Several times a month" were scored Medium; and those who responded "Once a month or less" or "Never" were scored Low.

is a reflection of the age of this inmate population and its place in society. The inmates are essentially still adolescents, who, for the most part, are not completely emancipated and independent of their parents. At the same time, like other adolescents, they are still very much peer-oriented. What we are seeing here may very well be a reflection of the adolescent inmate society, and the dynamics of this society apparently differ from that of adult inmate society. Whatever the dynamics, these findings clearly indicate that Hypothesis 2g needs to be revised, at least to the extent that it is to be applicable to this type of inmate population.

Integration and Inmate Adaptations

While the questions of the nature and extent of integration within the inmate group are legitimate topics of investigation in themselves, they are of special interest here because of the previously reported relationships found between integration and inmate attitudes, especially as they reflect the prisonization process. Hypothesis 3a and Hypothesis 3b deal with the relationships we would expect to find between integration and prisonization at our two organizational sites on the basis of our model of the alternate society and previous research on this topic.

Integration and Prisonization in Permissive and
Restrictive Organizational Climates

Hypothesis 3a *Integration in the inmate group in institutions characterized by a permissive climate will be related to nonprisonized orientations on the part of the inmates.*

Hypothesis 3b *Integration in the inmate group in institutions characterized by a restrictive organizational climate will be related to prisonized orientations on the part of the inmates.*

According to Hypotheses 3a and 3b we would expect integration to be negatively associated with prisonized orientations at Federal East and positively associated with prisonized orientations at Federal West. The data presented in Table 4-9 support the latter but not the former prediction.

Contrary to Hypothesis 3a there was a low *negative* relationship between integration and conformity at both institutions. The more integrated inmates were slightly less likely to give conforming responses than those inmates who were less integrated. In proposing Hypothesis 3a we had relied heavily on the previous findings of Street, who found integration related to conformity or nonprisonized responses in treatment-oriented institutions.[8] Our findings, however, more closely resemble those reported by Clemmer and Wheeler in their studies of adult institutions.[9]

At Federal West we found a low negative association between integration and conformity responses as had been hypothesized and as has been previously reported for several adult institutions. Hypothesis 3b appears to be our best generalization regarding the relationship between integration and conformity; to the extent that there is a relationship between integration and conformity, it will be an inverse relationship regardless of the organizational setting.

Given the fact that previous studies have rather consistently reported a significant relationship between integration and conformity orientations, the relationships we found between these variables appear to be surprisingly low. One possible explanation for the absence of a stronger relationship is that there are other factors that affect the relationship between integration and conformity. One such factor may be the ties the inmates maintain with

Table 4-9
Inmate Conformity Index Scores Controlled by Integration Index Scores
(percentages)

Conformity Index	Integration Index		
	Low	*Medium*	*High*
Federal East			
Low	12	5	16
Medium	38	42	48
High	50	53	36
	(68)	(43)	(44)
		$\gamma = -.14$	
Federal West			
Low	14	24	25
Medium	56	47	45
High	30	29	30
	(143)	(63)	(63)
		$\gamma = -.11$	

others outside of the institution. This is an area where a great deal of change has occurred regarding visits, letters, phone calls, and furloughs as well as higher standards of living and improved transportation facilities, all making possible and feasible increased contact between the inmate and family and friends outside the institution. Previous research has indicated that we could anticipate a relationship between the number of outside ties the inmate maintains and the extent to which he is integrated within the inmate group and between the number of outside ties and the extent to which he manifests conformity or prisonized orientations. We have already found earlier in our discussion of Hypothesis 2g, that, contrary to what we had predicted, there was a positive association between the number of contacts the inmate has with persons outside the institution and the extent to which he is integrated within the inmate group. To what extent are such contacts related to the conformity orientations? Table 4-10 addresses this question. Here we find a low positive relationship ($\gamma = +.18$) at Federal East between outside contacts and conformity; at Federal West we find a slightly stronger moderate positive relationship ($\gamma = +.23$) between these variables. The greater the amount of contact the inmate has with family and friends outside the institution the more likely he is to endorse norms of conduct endorsed by the staff. This finding affirms the earlier contention of Clemmer that prisonization is inversely related to contact with others outside the institution.[10]

Thus far we have found low or moderate *positive* associations between the number of outside contacts an inmate has and his conformity scores and

Table 4-10

Inmate Conformity Index Scores Controlled by Outside Contacts Index Scores

(percentages)

Conformity Index	Outside Contacts Index		
	Low	*Medium*	*High*
Federal East			
Low	12	10	13
Medium	44	55	32
High	44	35	55
	(25)	(52)	(79)
		$\gamma = +.18$	
Federal West			
Low	33	15	13
Medium	46	54	52
High	21	31	35
	(61)	(110)	(105)
		$\gamma = +.23$	

integration scores, and low *negative* associations between his integration scores and conformity scores. These associations are summarized in Table 4-11. As Table 4-11 clearly indicates, except for small variations in magnitude, the relationships between these three variables at the two organizations are very similar. There are low or moderate positive associations between outside contacts and both integration and conformity, but these associations are not strong enough to preclude a low negative association between integration and conformity at the two institutions.

The initial stimulus for this more detailed analysis was an interest in whether or not a third variable may have an impact on the relationship between integration and conformity. This question is addressed directly by the data presented in Table 4-12.

As can be seen in Table 4-12, controlling for the number of outside contacts an inmate had allows us to specify the conditions under which there is a relationship between integration and conformity. At Federal East there is virtually no relationship whatsoever between integration and conformity for those inmates who scored in the low or medium categories of the outside contacts index. Most of the overall low negative association ($\gamma = -.14$) between integration and conformity at Federal East was the result of the moderate negative association ($\gamma = -.25$) between these variables among those inmates who scored highest on the outside contacts index. A somewhat different picture emerges for Federal West, however. At Federal

Table 4-11
Associations between Outside Contacts, Integration, and Conformity at Federal East and Federal West
(gamma scores)

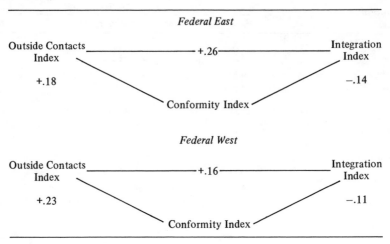

Table 4-12
Relationships between Integration and Conformity Controlling for Outside Contacts
(percentages)

	Outside Contacts Index								
	Low			*Medium*			*High*		
	Integration Index			*Integration Index*			*Integration Index*		
Conformity Index	*Low*	*Medium*	*High*	*Low*	*Medium*	*High*	*Low*	*Medium*	*High*
Federal East									
Low	15		17	15		8	7	9	19
Medium	47	17	66	47	64	67	29	29	35
High	38	83	17	38	36	25	64	64	46
	(13)	(6)	(6)	(26)	(14)	(12)	(28)	(28)	(26)
		$\gamma = -.02$			$\gamma = -.05$			$\gamma = -.25$	
Federal West									
Low	17	44	60	14	19	18	9	14	19
Medium	40	44	30	55	50	53	58	48	44
High	43	12	10	31	31	29	29	38	36
	(42)	(16)	(10)	(65)	(26)	(17)	(17)	(21)	(36)
		$\gamma = -.59$			$\gamma = -.05$			$\gamma = -.04$	

West there was virtually no relationship between integration and conformity for those inmates in the medium and high categories of the outside contacts measure, but there was a substantial negative association ($\gamma = -.59$) between these variables for those inmates who were low on outside contacts. Outside contacts affect the relationship between integration and conformity differently at the two organizational settings. At Federal West it appears that outside contacts have a neutralizing impact on the relationship between integration and conformity: when the inmates have few outside contacts there is a substantial negative association, but, when the number of outside contacts increase, that relationship all but disappears. Those inmates, who were low on outside contacts and highly integrated, are the most negative or prisonized of all the subgroups in Table 4-12.

Explaining the pattern found at Federal East is not quite so simple. Why should there be a moderate negative association between integration and conformity for those high on outside contacts but not for those with fewer outside contacts? Explaining this phenomenon requires speculation beyond the data and the introduction of some assumptions about a fourth variable that we have only been able to measure indirectly: the overall impact of staff and treatment program. At Federal East there was a very high staff-inmate ratio and a relatively intensive counseling program. In contrast, at Federal West the staff-inmate ratio was approximately half that at Federal East and only minimal resources were committed to the counseling program. It may be that intensive staff contact and counseling had an impact on both integrated and nonintegrated inmates alike among those inmates who had low or medium degrees of outside contact, but that this influence was weakened somewhat by competing sources of influence among those inmates who had the most outside contacts. Whether or not the latter group of inmates was integrated within the inmate group became a salient factor associated with their conformity orientations. In other words, outside contacts diluted the impact of staff and treatment programs, and an association between conformity and integration emerged under these conditions. A different pattern existed at Federal West due to the relative absence of staff contact and counseling programs. In any case, too much should not be made of the negative relationship between integration and conformity among the high contact inmates at Federal East, since this relationship is only moderate ($\gamma = -.25$) in strength and these inmates, who are high on outside contacts and high on integration, are more positive in their conformity responses than any other group of inmates other than those in the high outside contacts category.

Having reviewed the relationship of integration and conformity under varying degrees of outside contacts, we can conclude that whatever relationship exists at either institution is negative and that this relationship exists only under certain conditions, which differ from institution to institution:

there was a moderate negative relationship under a condition of high outside contact at Federal East and a substantial negative relationship under a condition of low outside contacts at Federal West.

Integration and Pluralistic Ignorance

Hypothesis 3c *The accuracy of the inmate's perception of the orientations of other inmates will be related to integration within the inmate group.*

In Chapter 2 we noted the relatively common finding that inmates tend to believe that other inmates have less commitment to staff-supported values than is the case as revealed by the privately expressed values of the inmates themselves. We argued there that such misperceptions are related to the quality and quantity of communication the inmate receives and that such communication is a function of the extent to which the inmate is integrated into the inmate group. The more integrated the inmate, the greater the quantity of communication he receives and the more open the quality of this communication, resulting in more accurate perceptions of the values and norms held by others.

A technique similar to that previously used by Wheeler was utilized to measure the concept of "pluralistic ignorance."[11] At the same time that the inmates were presented with the vignettes used in constructing the conformity index they were asked, in addition to whether or not they approved of the action taken, how many other inmates would approve of such an action. By comparing the number that various groups of inmates believed would approve an action with the number of inmates who actually did approve, we could estimate the extent to which various groups misperceived or manifested "pluralistic ignorance" of the values actually held by their fellow inmates. Table 4-13 presents the percent of those who actually approved of the action taken in the vignette, the estimate by the inmates of the percent of all inmates who would approve, and the estimate by inmates of varying degrees of integration of the percent of all inmates who would approve.

There are a number of observations to be made regarding the data in Table 4-13. One of the most striking findings is the consistency and the extent to which the inmates clearly underestimate the proportion of other inmates who endorse staff-approved or prosocial norms of conduct. For all five situations and at both institutions the inmates consistently underestimate the proportion of their fellow inmates who approve of the prosocial alternative of action, sometimes by as much as 40 percent. Some differences do exist between the institutions in this regard, however. The discrepancy between the percent who actually approved and the percent that

Table 4-13

Accuracy of Inmate Perceptions of Role Expectations Controlled by Integration
(percentages)

		Estimates of Those Approving by[a]			
Situation[b]	*Percent Actually Approving*	*All Inmates*	*Low Integration*	*Medium Integration*	*High Integration*
Federal East					
Escape	62	51	50	<u>60</u>	44
Work detail	83	49	46	<u>61</u>	46
Money	58	72	73	<u>69</u>	70
Job classi- fication	24	59	66	58	<u>52</u>
Rule Infrac- tion	62	37	34	<u>44</u>	34
Federal West					
Escape	35	19	20	<u>24</u>	11
Work detail	86	43	41	<u>45</u>	42
Money	70	88	89	88	<u>83</u>
Job Classi- fication	33	63	<u>62</u>	66	<u>62</u>
Rule Infrac- tion	50	14	<u>14</u>	12	<u>14</u>

[a]Underlined estimates are those closest to the percent actually approving.

[b]See pages 51-52 for a description of the situations presented.

all the inmates estimated would approve is greater for four of the five items at Federal West. In other words, pluralistic ignorance is more prevalent in the restrictive than the permissive organizational climate. It also appears that integration bears more of a relationship to the accuracy of the inmates' perceptions at Federal East than at Federal West. The range of the estimates of those who would approve by the low, medium, and high integration inmates at Federal West equals or exceeds ten percentage points in only one instance; at Federal East the range of the estimates of those who would approve by the low, medium, and high integration inmates equals or exceeds ten percentage points in four out of five instances. Not only is there little variation in the estimates by inmates of varying degrees of integration, but there also is little relationship between integration and accuracy of perception at Federal West. The estimates of the low integration inmates approximate the percent actually approving about as often as the medium and high integration inmates. At Federal East there was not only greater variation in the responses by inmates of varying degrees of integration, but there was also more of a relationship between integration and the accuracy of the inmate's perception of the stand to be taken by others; for four of the five situations the estimates of those who were moderately integrated were the most accurate; on the remaining situation the high integration inmates were most accurate in their estimates. The low integration inmates were not once closest in their estimates of the percentage of others who would approve of a certain course of action. It may be that for such matters being moderately integrated has certain advantages in that one is neither isolated nor locked into a group but can more readily gauge the positions of others.

Overall, however, the data do not support Hypothesis 3c as it was stated. We had predicted a direct relationship between integration and the accuracy of the inmates' perceptions. At Federal West we found little variation in the perceptions of inmates of varying degrees of integration and no consistent pattern between integration and accuracy of perception. At Federal East we found considerable variation in perceptions, but it was the moderately integrated rather than the highly integrated inmates who were most accurate in their perceptions of the norms endorsed by others. Once again we find that the meaning of integration varies from organizational setting to organizational setting and that attempts to specify the relationship between integration and pluralistic ignorance must take account of the larger organizational context.

Summary

Our first set of hypotheses dealt with the relationships between the organizational climate and background characteristics of inmates and the extent to which the inmates were prisonized. The most significant finding from our examination of these variables was that the background of the inmates, measured in terms of previous involvement in law violations was more strongly related to the conformity responses of the inmates than was the organizational climate in which the inmate was located. For those inmates who had not been involved in previous offense incidents or who had been involved in very few, the organizational setting was important. But for those whose records showed four or more previous offense incidents, the organizational setting made little difference. Thus it appears that the deprivation model provides us with a valid explanation of the prisonization phenomenon for those inmates who have not previously been deeply involved in violating the law; while for those who have numerous offenses, the importation model may be more appropriate.

In examining our second set of hypotheses we found, as we had predicted, that the inmates at Federal East tended to be more integrated than the inmates at Federal West. Contrary to our hypothesis, we found a low to moderate positive association between the frequency of the inmate's outside contacts and integration within the inmate group. A number of researchers who had studied older inmate populations stated that they had found a negative relationship between these variables. We found that it is not an either/or situation. It may be that the dynamics of the inmate groups we are studying conform more closely to the dynamics of an adolescent peer society rather than those of an older adult prison population.

Our third set of hypotheses dealt with the relationships between integration and inmate attitudes and perceptions. Contrary to the reports of previous research we found little association between integration and prisonized responses on the part of the inmates. The major exception to this statement was the case of the inmates at Federal West who had only infrequent outside contacts. For these inmates there was a substantial negative association between integration and prisonized responses.

These then are what we consider to be the major findings of the chapter. We will discuss their policy implications in Chapter 7. We will examine more closely the actual friendship patterns that prevailed at the two institutions in Chapter 5.

Notes

1. Denton Morrison and Ramon Hershel, *The Significance Test Controversy—A Reader* (Chicago: Aldine Publishing Co., 1970).

2. John Mueller, Karl Schuessler, and Herbert Costner, *Statistical Reasoning in Sociology*, 2d ed. (Boston: Houghton Mifflin Co., 1970).

3. Donald Clemmer, *The Prison Community* (New York: Holt, Rinehart and Winston, 1958), p. 299.

4. Stanton Wheeler, "Social Organization in a Correctional Community" (Ph.D. dissertation, University of Washington, 1958).

5. Ibid., pp. 170-215.

6. Daniel Glaser, *The Effectiveness of a Prison and Parole System* (Indianapolis:Bobbs-Merril Co., 1964), pp. 89-118.

7. Ibid., pp. 89-98.

8. David Street, "Inmate Social Organization: A Comparative Study of Juvenile Correctional Institutions" (Ph.D. dissertation, University of Michigan, 1962), pp. 85-91.

9. Clemmer, *Prison Community*, pp. 298-304; and Wheeler, "Social Organization in Correctional Community," pp. 187, 203-215.

10. Clemmer, *Prison Community*, pp. 298-304.

11. The procedure for measuring "pluralistic ignorance" was adopted directly from Wheeler's study, "Social Organization in a Correctional Com-

munity," pp. 65-66. For each of the vignettes presented, the inmates were asked:

How many guys here do you think would approve (of the behavior of the inmate in the situation)?

Almost All	About three-fourths	About half	About one-fourth	Almost none
( )	( )	( )	( )	( )

The median estimate rather than the mean is used as a measure of central tendency, since the distributions of perception responses are in several cases highly skewed. To compute a median percentage for each group it is necessary to make assumptions about the mid-points and widths of the intervals between the five response categories. This computation becomes somewhat simplified if we assume that the extreme categories of "Almost all" and "Almost none" have an interval width half the size of the middle three categories. The mid-points of the three middle categories are suggested by the wording of the items, i.e., 75 percent, 50 percent, and 25 percent respectively. Given an interval width of 25 percent for the middle categories, the extreme categories then have a width of 12.5 percent. The interval range and mid-point for each response category then becomes

Almost all: upper limit, 100 percent; lower limit, 87.5 percent; mid-point, 93.75 percent

About three-fourths: upper limit, 87.5 percent; lower limit, 62.5 percent; mid-point, 75 percent

About one-fourth: upper limit, 37.5 percent; lower limit, 12.5 percent; mid-point, 25 percent

Almost none: upper limit, 12.5 percent; lower limit, 00.0 percent; mid-point, 6.25 percent.

By use of this scoring system it is possible to translate the responses of a set of respondents into a median percentage estimate of how others feel about each situation. It then becomes possible to compare how inmates feel about a situation with the general perceptions of how they feel about that situation.

5

Interpersonal Relations within the Alternate Society: Empirical Findings

In this chapter we turn our attention to consideration of the fourth set of hypotheses presented in Chapter 2: Hypotheses 4a through 4d, Interpersonal Relations within the Alternate Society. We will be reviewing the reports of the inmates regarding those they consider to be their friends and attempting to determine what social factors affect or place parameters around the selection of others as friends within the inmate group.

Methodological Notes

Before beginning a substantive discussion of the questions mentioned above, it is appropriate to discuss the statistical measures to be used in summarizing and evaluating the relationships to be reported. The basic question that underlies most of the hypotheses to be examined in this chapter and the next is that of the extent to which inmates choose friends or nominate leaders who are similar to themselves in terms of certain basic characteristics. In other words, to what extent are friendship and leadership nominations made on an intraclass basis rather than an interclass basis in terms of such characteristics as living unit, age, and race? We can, of course, begin to answer this question by comparing the number of *intra*class choices with the number of *inter*class choices made by the inmates. Such a comparison, however, still leaves us with two other questions:

1. What is the relative strength of the tendency of the inmates to make intraclass choices rather than interclass choices for different characteristics?
2. Given the distribution among the inmates of the characteristics being studied, how likely is it that the relationship found may be due solely to chance?

To answer these questions, we have decided to utilize a statistical procedure widely used during the heyday of sociometric studies in the early 1940s: Criswell's index of self-preference.

Criswell presented an index of self-preference, which is a double ratio measure based on the distribution of sociometric choices to be expected on the basis of chance.[1] By dividing the *observed* ratio of in-group choices to out-group choices by the *expected* ratio of in-group choices to out-group choices she arrived at an intensity score that indicated how many times greater or less than chance were the self-preferences of various groups. The measure has the advantages of being independent of group size and percentage composition, and the reciprocal of the self-preference score constitutes an index of other-group preference.

A second measure to be used in examining the data relevant to several of the hypotheses in this chapter and in the next is an index that measures the similarity between two inmates on nine variables simultaneously. The index scores for a pair of inmates range from 0, not at all similar, to 9, similar on all nine variables. In calculating the Similarity Index we controlled for the effect of proximity by examining only the similarity scores of the inmates and their friends and of the inmates and nonfriends within individual living units and obtained a composite score by summing across living units within each institution. An inmate was considered very similar to a friend or a non-friend if the similarity score for the pairing was 5 or larger. Inmates were scored as similar if they were classified within the same categories of each variable. The following variables and categories were used for this index.

Age: 18 and below, 19, 20, 21 and above

Race: White, Black, Indian and Other

Social Class: Lower, Middle, Upper

No. of Previous Offenses: None (0), Few (1-3), Many (4+)

Type of Offense: Public Order, Property, Person-Oriented

Previous Institutionalization: None, Some

Length of Stay: 1-3 mos., 4-6 mos., 7-12 mos., 13+ mos.

No. of Misconduct Reports: None, One or more

No. of Times in Segregation: None, One or more

Any inmate who chose a friend outside of his living unit, or for whom data on one of our comparisons were missing, was excluded from the index.

Interpersonal Relations within the Alternate Society

In Chapter 2 we briefly reviewed a number of hypotheses regarding the factors likely to affect the friendship choices of the inmates at Federal East and Federal West. Before actually examining the responses of the inmates, it is appropriate to pause briefly to discuss the concept of "friendship." What specifically are we asking the inmates when we ask them who their friends are? To define friends as others who they "like" or who they are "attracted to'' or "whom they would like to spend time with'' provides us with part but not the entire answer to our question. One of the basic rules of sociometric measurement is that subjects should be asked to choose their friends in terms of specific criteria or activities. We can expect respondents to choose different persons for instrumental and for expressive activities. Ultimately then, the question becomes that of how the concept of friendship was operationalized for this book.

To study the friendship relations that existed among our inmate respondents we asked them to name two other inmates they would like to have accompany them on a short leave from the institution. Specifically they were asked: "If you had a chance to make a town trip, what two guys from here would you choose to go with you?'' While the question was a hypothetical one, it was also realistic, since many inmates were eligible for town trips, and all were familiar with them. The question also focused the respondent's attention on those inmates he would like to be with for socioemotional rather than task-related reasons.

Of the 176 inmates at Federal East, 131 (75 percent) responded to the above question by naming two choices, 20 (11 percent) named only one choice, and 25 (14 percent) did not name any other inmates. At Federal West 220 (71 percent) of the 312 inmates named two choices, 42 (13 percent) named only óne choice, and 50 (16 percent) did not name any other inmates. Thus, almost 85 percent of the inmates at both institutions were willing to name at least one other inmate as someone they would have accompany them on a town trip. This response rate was a very good one, especially for a correctional setting and was probably due to (1) the basically innocuous wording of the question, and (2) the credibility that the researchers were able to establish with the inmates at the two institutions.

The distributions of friendship choices at the two institutions were strikingly similar, although the choices were somewhat more dispersed at Federal West, where there were proportionately slightly fewer inmates who received no town trip choices (28 percent compared to 34 percent at Federal East) and slightly more who received one or two choices. Very few inmates, less than 5 percent, received more than four town trip choices at either institution.

A preliminary analysis of the data indicated that the patterning of the inmates' first and second town trip choices was very similar, consequently we chose to base our analysis only on the inmates' first town trip choice, thereby avoiding both the data overload that would result from the presentation of the two choices separately and the disproportionate weighting of some inmates' responses that would result from a pooled presentation of both the first and second choices. This, then was the data set we used to examine our hypotheses regarding interpersonal relations among the inmates at Federal East and Federal West.

Friendship Choices and Propinquity

Hypotheses 4a *Friendship choices among the inmates will vary with propinquity or physical proximity.*

There is a fairly extensive body of literature documenting the importance of propinquity or physical proximity in the friendship process. Hare, after reviewing a large number of studies, went on to describe proximity as the first filter in a funnel that determines who becomes friends with whom.[2] Similarly, Lindzey and Byrne after an extensive review of the literature concluded that friendship choice varies with propinquity.[3] The more accessible two people are to each other, the greater the potential for their interaction. This accessibility makes possible a process that Kipnis described as "such that as two men interact with each other more and more, they begin to seem more likeable to each other."[4]

If propinquity is of such importance in general society, we would expect it to be of even greater importance within the correctional institution, where contacts among inmates are restricted by schedules and regulations. At both Federal East and Federal West the constraints of dealing with large numbers of inmates within certain limits of security often required the handling of the inmates in groups. The most basic of these groups were the living unit or cottage groupings.

Table 5-1 presents the data bearing on Hypothesis 4a.

In this table we have compared the number of choices within each living unit which would be expected (E) if choice were not related to living unit with those actually observed (0). The last column to the right in Table 5-1 contains the ratio of self-preference scores for each of the living units. The ratio of self-preference (the ratio of observed in-group choices to out-group choices divided by the ratio of expected in-group choices to expected out-group choices) indicates the factor by which the observed proportion of in-group choices is greater than or less than that expected on the basis of chance. A self-preference ratio of 1.00 would indicate that the group members chose each other as often as would be expected on the basis of chance; a self-preference ratio of .5 would indicate that they chose each other half as often as would be expected on the basis of chance; a self-preference ratio of 2.00 would indicate that they chose each other twice as often as would be expected on the basis of chance alone.

An examination of Table 5-1 indicates that there was a very strong tendency for the inmates to choose their town trip partners from among the other members of their own living unit. At Federal East, for instance, the inmates in Unit 2 chose other inmates from that unit as their town trip companions 57.8 times more often than would be expected on the basis of their numbers in the overall population. Even in Unit 1 at Federal East,

Table 5-1
Relationship between Town Trip Choices and Living Unit

Living Unit of Chooser	Living Unit of Chosen										Total	Ratio of Self-Preference
	Unit 1		Unit 2		Unit 3		Unit 4		Unit 5			
	O	E	O	E	O	E	O	E	O	E		
Federal East												
Unit 1	29	9.73	2	6.34	0	4.65	2	9.09	4	7.19	37	10.2
Unit 2	0	6.71	23	4.14	0	3.14	0	6.14	2	4.86	25	57.8
Unit 3	0	4.30	0	2.74	14	1.92	2	3.93	0	3.11	16	51.5
Unit 4	1	11.01	0	7.03	1	5.15	36	9.84	3	7.97	41	22.8
Unit 5	2	8.33	1	5.31	1	3.90	4	7.62	23	5.85	31	12.4
Sum											150	

Living Unit of Chooser	Living Unit of Chosen								Total	Ratio of Self-Preference
	Unit 1		Unit 2		Unit 3		Unit 4			
	O	E	O	E	O	E	O	E		
Federal West[a]										
Unit 1	35	13.76	7	14.91	6	12.04	4	11.28	52	5.7
Unit 2	6	15.30	42	16.14	6	13.20	3	12.36	57	7.1
Unit 3	7	13.69	5	14.62	37	11.62	2	11.06	51	9.0
Unit 4	6	11.27	3	12.04	4	9.73	29	8.96	42	8.2
Sum									202	

[a]Excludes chooser and chosen inmates from work release and special treatment living units.

where the tendency to choose within the living unit was weakest, the self-preference ratio is 10.2. The tendency to choose one's friends from within one's own living unit at first seems somewhat unevenly distributed at Federal East. The self-preference ratios of Unit 2 and Unit 3 are 57.8 and 51.5 respectively; the self-preference ratios of Units 1, 4, and 5 are 10.2, 22.8, and 12.4 respectively. These differences, however, can be explained by the fact that Unit 5 was constituted shortly before the data were gathered, and a number of inmates who had previously resided in Unit 1 or Unit 4 were transferred into the new unit. Therefore, it is not surprising that the residents of these three living units would have manifested a greater tendency to choose their friends across the currently existing living unit boundaries. What is less obvious is why the self-preference ratios at Federal West should be so much smaller than those obtained at Federal East. At Federal West the self-preference ratios range from 5.7 to 9.0 for the living units examined. The largest of these ratios, 9.0, is still less than the smallest ratio at Federal East, 10.2. Given the greater emphasis on mass handling and standardization at Federal West, we would have predicted that the opposite would have been true. It may be that there were other factors influencing the choices of the inmates at Federal West which reduced the relative importance of propinquity. It is more likely, however, that we had underestimated the importance of the cottage-based treatment program and other activities at Federal East in fostering an identification with the cottage group. Unfortunately we lack comparable data for other institutions, which might allow us to decide whether the self-preference ratios found at Federal West were unusually low or whether the self-preference ratios at Federal East were unusually high. Overall, however, we must conclude that friendship choices as manifested by our town trip question were living-unit-based to a greater extent at Federal East than at Federal West.

Friendship Choices and Personal, Offense, and
Organizational Characteristics

Hypothesis 4b *Inmates will tend to choose as friends other inmates who are similar to themselves in terms of various personal, offense, and organizational characteristics.*

Hypothesis 4c *The friendship choices of inmates in restrictive organizational climates will show a greater tendency to be structured according to personal, offense, and organizational categories than the friendship choices of inmates in permissive organizational climates.*

Recognizing the interrelatedness of Hypotheses 4b and 4c, we will consider them simultaneously as we examine the relevant data. In considering these hypotheses we will examine first the Similarity Index described above, which is based on nine variables, and then go on to examine the self-preference ratios of the inmates for each of the nine variables individually. These nine variables are (1) the personal characteristics of age, race, and social class; (2) the offense characteristics of the number of previous offenses, type of commitment offense, and whether or not the inmate was previously institutionalized; and (3) the organizationally assigned characteristics of length of stay, number of major misconduct reports, and the number of times the inmates had been in segregation. We will explicate our rationale for including each of the variables in our analysis when we discuss the self-preference ratios of the inmates for each of these variables. For the present we note that we see similarity on these variables indicating that the inmates had had certain experiences which had the potential of generating common interests and orientations. Hypothesis 4c, however, states a relationship to characterize the state of affairs in the two institutions for all of these variables, and it would be best if we further explicated that argument before moving on. According to Hypothesis 4c, the friendship choices at Federal West, which had a more restrictive organizational climate than Federal East, should more often be structured along categorical lines than the friendship choices at Federal East, which had a more permissive climate. Basically, the argument here is that those factors which contribute to and result from the more restrictive climate at Federal West (emphasis on custody, social distance between staff and inmates, limited gratifications, predatory relationships among inmates) will result in inmates relying on more basic, although superficial, indicators of whom it is safe to associate with as a friend. Rather than being open to accepting as friends all others and exploring the possibility of very particularistic bases for friendship, the inmates at Federal West should more often limit their friendship choices to those who are similar to themselves in terms of such manifest characteristics as race and age. At Federal East the more permissive organizational climate will make possible more openness among inmates of different backgrounds, allowing for friendship choices based on something other than manifest gross characteristics.

Similarity Index Scores. One way of approaching Hypotheses 4b and 4c is to ask whether the inmates chose as friends other inmates who were more like themselves than the inmates they did not choose as friends. We can do this by determining whether similarity in terms of nine selected variables was greater among friends than nonfriends, without attempting to identify those variables for which similarity was not important. The question here is one of degree of similarity rather than kind of similarity. We will attempt to begin to answer the latter question in the sections which follow.

The Similarity Index described at the beginning of the chapter allows us to examine pair relationships within living units at each institution. The Similarity Index scores ranged from 0 to 9, and those pairs of inmates whose scores were 5 or greater were considered very similar. The Similarity Index scores were dichotomized into Not Very Similar (0-4) and Very Similar (5-9). Five was chosen as the lower limit for the Very Similar category since it was the middle point of the nine points on the index and also because this category contained the median case in the distribution of index scores at Federal East and was the category next to the one which contained the median case at Federal West. Table 5-2 presents the distribution of the percentage of very similar pairings among friends and nonfriends (all others in the living unit) at Federal East and Federal West.

The data in Table 5-2 support both Hypotheses 4b and 4c. At both Federal East and Federal West the percentage of friendship pairings in the very similar category was greater than the pairings between the inmates who chose friends and their nonfriends. Over all similarity was relevant for friendship choices.

Table 5-2
Distribution of Very Similar Pairs among Friends and Nonfriends
(percentages)

	Between Chooser and Friend	Between Chooser and Nonfriends[a]
Federal East	75 $(101)^b$	62 $(3216)^c$
Federal West	66 $(114)^b$	36 $(6500)^c$

[a]Nonfriends are all the other inmates in the living unit for which the full complement of data was available.

[b]This is the number of within-living-unit friendship pairs for which index scores were available in the institution.

[c]This is the number of possible within-living-unit pairings of choosers with those they did not choose and for whom index scores were available in the institution.

At Federal East 75 percent of the friendship pairings were very similar, while 62 percent of the nonfriendship pairings were very similar—a difference of 13 percentage points. At Federal West 66 percent of the friendship pairings were very similar, while 36 percent of the nonfriendship pairings were very similar—a difference of 30 percentage points. On the basis of these observations we may conclude that similarity was a more important factor in friendship choices at Federal West.

Personal Characteristics. Before examining empirically the relevance of similarity of personal characteristics at the two institutions, let us briefly review why we should expect this to be related to the friendship choices of the inmates.

We previously cited Hare's conceptualization of proximity as the first filter in a funnel that serves to narrow the range of persons who are likely to become one's friends. For Hare the second filter in the funnel analogy is similarity of personal characteristics:

Persons who choose each other tend to have *similar individual characteristics*, such as age, intelligence, sex, and athletic ability (Furfey, 1927; Parten, 1933b; Richardson, 1939; Smith, 1944; Faunce & Beegle, 1948; James, 1951b), although an occasional study reports no association between these variables and friendship formation (Bonney, 1946).[5]

Lindzey and Byrne in their review of the literature on interpersonal attraction likewise concluded that:

Not only is sociometric status found to be related to demographic variables such as socio-economic status, religion, sex, and age, but similarity in these characteristics apparently leads to interpersonal attraction.[6]

Theodore Newcomb in *The Acquaintance Process* also reported finding a relationship between certain "quasi-demographic variables" and interpersonal attraction and interpreted these variables as indicators or at least perceived indicators of common orientations, which he saw as the basis of friendship relationships.

We also found that pair similarity with regard to certain objective, quasi-demographic variables predicted to early pair attraction—and also, in one population, to later attraction. The total set of findings is consistent with the interpretation that the predictive power of pair similarity of these kinds inheres in the common orientations that are likely to be associated with similarity of environment, or that are assumed to be associated with them.[7]

Among these quasi-demographic variables were age, college environment, religious preference, urban-rural background, and room assignment.

It is on the basis of this earlier theoretical and empirical work that we have hypothesized that similarity in terms of the personal characteristics of age, race, and social class would be an important determinant of the friendship choices of the inmates at Federal East and Federal West.

Age. After placing the inmates into four age categories—18 and below, 19, 20, and 21 and above—and examining the self-preference ratios of the inmates we concluded that there was little relationship between similarity of age and town trip choice at either Federal East or Federal West. The inmates' choice patterns closely resembled those to be expected on the basis of chance. Most of the ratios of self-preference were very close to unity. The major exceptions to this statement were the "21 and above" groups at both institutions. These inmates chose other inmates of their own age category more than twice as often as would be expected on the basis of chance. The age of 21 is a milestone age in American society, and it may be that this age had a qualitative meaning above and beyond its quantitative meaning for these inmates. Twenty-one is the age of majority in many states, and its attainment carries with it many rights and privileges denied to those of younger ages. The fact that, with the exception of the "21 and above" groups, we found little relationship between age and sociometric choice is not altogether surprising given the narrow range of ages in our study populations. The large majority of the inmates at both Federal East and Federal West were either 18, 19, or 20 years old, and there is little reason to expect much differentiation in friendship choices among those who have in common the advantages and disadvantages of late adolescence. The fact that there was a tendency toward self-preference among the "21 and above" inmates does indicate that although a mere difference in years may not always be important, the qualitative meanings associated with certain ages may be related to friendship patterns. At both institutions, men (21 and above) more often chose other men (21 and above) than boys (20 and below) as their town trip choices. Overall, however, age did not seem to have been a strong determining factor in the sociometric choices of the inmates.

Given the absence of a clear relationship between the age of those inmates choosing and those inmates chosen at both of the institutions, there is no basis for concluding that friendship choices were more often structured along categorical lines at either institution. Similarity of ages appears to have been equally important or not important at Federal East and Federal West.

Race. Examining the self-preference ratios of white, black, and Indian categories of inmates, we found that race was a very important factor affecting friendship choices. The smallest self-preference ratio, that of whites at Federal East, was 3.7, indicating that white inmates chose other white inmates almost four times as often as they would have been expected to if they were making their choices in proportion to the number of whites in the overall inmate population. The ratios of self-preference of the minority groups, the blacks (19.2) at Federal East and the blacks (35.4) and Indians (20.7) at Federal West, indicated an even higher degree of ethnic closure in friendships than was found for the whites at either institution. Also noteworthy was the pattern of choices of the two minority groupings at Federal West. Blacks chose other blacks, and in a few instances blacks chose whites; there was not a single instance of a black having chosen an Indian as a friend. Similarly, our Indian respondents chose primarily other Indians and a few whites; there was not a single instance of an Indian having chosen a black as a friend. Why should this be so? We cannot offer a definitive explanation for this phenomenon. Observations and interviews had led us to expect animosity among the three racial groups at the institution, but there was little reason to expect the pattern we did find. It might be that when a member of a minority chooses a friend outside of his own group, the tendency is to select a person of higher status rather than a person who is a member of another minority group. In other words, what may be indicated here is a process of "status-seeking" through friendship choices. However, whatever the explanation may be for this specific phenomenon, we conclude rather firmly that race was a very important factor influencing sociometric choices within these correctional settings.

These data provide support for Hypothesis 4c. Overall there was more closure of friendship choices along ethnic lines at Federal West than at Federal East. The self-preference ratios of whites at Federal East was 3.7; at Federal West it was 5.8. The self-preference ratio for blacks was 19.2 at Federal East; at Federal West it was 35.4. In sum, town trip choices were more often made according to racial categories at Federal West than at Federal East.

Social Class. The social class of the inmates was categorized as being lower, middle, or upper on the basis of the occupation of the chief wage earner in the inmate's family. (Lower class included private household workers, service workers, laborers, farmers, farm laborers, unemployed, welfare recipients; middle class included sales, clerical, craftsmen, foremen, operative, and kindred workers; and upper class included professional, technical, managers, officials, proprietors, and kindred workers.) The ratios of self-preference for all categories at both institutions exceeded unity, but in no instance did they exceed a factor of two.

Overall there appeared to be only a very weak tendency on the part of the inmates to choose others as their friends on the basis of social class similarity. The small and varying directions of the differences in the self-preference ratio scores at the two institutions prevent us from concluding that social class similarity was more salient for the inmates at one institution than at the other.

Offense Characteristics. In examining the relationship between similarity of offenses and friendship choices several caveats should be kept in mind. Here as elsewhere reference to the offense of the inmate refers to the inmate's officially recorded "instant" or commitment offense, and the number of previous offenses the inmate committed refers to the number of offenses which were actually recorded. Previous research has found that officially recorded delinquency statistics may be very poor indicators of delinquent behavior as determined through self-reports. Erickson and Empey concluded, for instance, that the dichotomy between official nondelinquents and one-time offenders did not prove to be discriminating as indicators of the total amount of delinquent behavior in which they engaged.[8] Gold, utilizing a variety of computer-implemented clustering techniques, was unable to locate any meaningful offender types among over 500 adolescents who were interviewed, indicating that the commitment offense of the official delinquents may be a very poor indicator of the other types of offenses the youths committed.[9]

Despite the problems associated with utilizing official offense records as indicators of delinquent behavior, we have chosen to include similarity of offense characteristics in our analysis for a number of reasons. Although Erickson and Empey found several of the commonly accepted dichotomies based on official records to be nondiscriminating, they concluded that court records, when compared with reported behavior, did distinguish persistent offenders from one-time offenders or nondelinquents, in terms of both number and seriousness of offense. Gold also reported a relationship between the number of delinquent acts and the number of times a youth's behavior was officially recorded as a delinquency. Therefore the number of previous offenses an inmate is recorded as having committed may be taken as a relative indicator of the number of delinquent acts, detected and undetected, he has committed. We believe that the inmates who have had more experience violating the law and being processed as law violators will choose as friends other inmates who are also more experienced in these areas.

We will also examine the utility of similarity of offense types in predicting friendship choices. While Gold reported finding no reliable offense types among his respondents, it appears that the inmates currently being studied differ from Gold's sample significantly in terms of a variable we believe may be related to offense patterns: age. Gold did not find any regular offender types among the 13 to 16 year respondents which comprised his sample. While our study does include some inmates who were sixteen and younger, they constituted less than 8 percent of the inmate populations at the two institutions. We believe that more stable offense patterns will be related to the age of offenders and that while young adolescents will engage in delinquency more or less as a "pickup game,"[10] older offenders will develop more stable patterns of offenses. Further, we would argue that the types of categories used to classify offense types will be related to the utility of one's typology. The categories used should be chosen in such a manner as to distinguish important groupings within the inmate population. In classifying offenses in the categories of Public Order, Property, and Person-Oriented we believe we will be making relevant distinctions among the inmates. For instance, at both Federal East and Federal West there were inmates whom we have classified as Public Order Offenders. This category was comprised primarily of drug offenders, many of whom were convicted of offenses involving the possession, transportation, or sale of marijuana, and Selective Service violators many of whom had refused to cooperate with the Selective Service System because of religious convictions. There is good reason to believe that these inmates shared certain common interests and values with each other that were not shared with other inmates to the same degree.

In addition to the above arguments, the work of Irwin also leads us to believe that similarity in terms of offense characteristics will be related to friendship choices among inmates. Irwin in his analysis of different modes of "doing time" argues that we can expect to find thieves participating in close-knit friendship groups with other thieves, but relatively uninvolved with others in the institution. Likewise, those identified as "dope fiends and heads" tend to form tight-knit friendship bonds with other "dope fiends and heads," although they generally participate also in larger circles of more casual friendships.[11] Similar offense backgrounds may be indicators of similar kinds of interests and experiences, which may in turn serve as a basis for the friendship relationship.

The relationship between similarity of experience in other institutions and friendship choices will also be examined. We believe that the official record of previous institutionalization is a reliable and valid indicator of this variable and that inmates who have had previous institutional experience will tend to choose as friends other inmates who are also experienced.

Number of Previous Offenses. We classified the inmates into three groups on the basis of the number of their previous offenses: None, Few (1-3), and Many (4 or more). With one exception the self-preference ratios of these groups closely approximated unity. At Federal West the inmates with no previous offenses tended to overselect other inmates like themselves. The ratio of self-preference for this group was 6.2, far exceeding the ratios of the other subgroups. These statistics, however, must be read with extreme caution because of the relatively small number of inmates (18) in the "None" category at Federal West. Nevertheless, it does appear that at least for a small subgroup of inmates, those with no previous offenses at Federal West, similarity in terms of previous offenses was related to friendship choice, although this did not hold true for the other two subgroups at Federal West nor for any of the subgroups at Federal East.

In relationship to Hypothesis 4c, these data provided little support that similarity in terms of number of previous offenses was more important at Federal West than at Federal East. It is important to note, however, that this *was* the case for the subgroup of inmates who had no previous offenses. Of all the subgroups, the inmates in the "None" category at Federal West were the only ones who showed a distinct tendency to make in-group choices.

Type of Offense. We classified the commitment offenses of the inmates into the three categories of Public Order (delinquency, Selective Service, drug offenses), Property (all forms of theft not involving a threat to a person), and Person-Oriented (all offenses involving a threat or actual assault on a person). There were too few inmates in the Person-Oriented category at Federal East to allow analysis of the friendship choices of these inmates. We found that the type of offense which led to the inmate's commitment to the institution was related to the inmate's friendship choices. At both institutions the friendship choices of the Public Order offenders departed substantially from the theoretically expected distributions.

The ratios of self-preference for the Public Order offenders were 11.9 at Federal East and 14.1 at Federal West. The ratios of self-preference are close to unity for the Property offenders: 1.3 and 1.4 at Federal East and Federal West respectively. At Federal West those inmates who had committed Person-Oriented offenses showed a greater tendency toward choosing their own kind than the Property offenders; the self-preference ratio of the inmates who had committed Person-Oriented offenses was 3.8. In sum, the data revealed a distinct tendency for the Public Order offenders to choose friends who were similar to themselves in terms of the type of offense which led to their commitment. A somewhat similar although less intense tendency also was evident in the choices of the Person-Oriented offenders at Federal West. The Property offenders at both institutions were less in-group oriented. Overall it does appear that the inmates at Federal West were more likely than those at Federal East to choose as friends other inmates who had committed types of crimes that were similar to the crimes that had led to their commitment.

Previous Institutionalization. In most instances at both institutions, whether or not an inmate had been previously institutionalized did not seem to be related to whether or not his town trip choice had been previously institutionalized. Inmates were classified into two groups on this variable: those who had not been previously institutionalized and those who had been previously institutionalized. For those inmates at Federal West who had been previously institutionalized and for those inmates at Federal East, whether or not they had been previously institutionalized, the self-preference ratios approximated unity. The inmates at Federal West who had not been previously institutionalized did show a slight preference for friends with a similar background in terms of this characteristic; their self-preference ratio of 1.6 was the highest of the subgroups. It is reasonable to expect that this characteristic—whether or not an inmate had been previously institutionalized—would be of greater relevance at Federal West than at Federal East. A greater proportion of the inmates at Federal West than at Federal East had been previously institutionalized and had spent time in institutions that had reputations as being "tough places." Consequently, having or not having been previously committed was of greater importance at Federal West. Those who were not previously institutionalized tended to choose others who had not been previously institutionalized, while this characteristic did not seem to make a difference in the choices of those who had been previously institutionalized.

Organizational Characteristics. In this section we will consider whether or not the inmates at Federal East and Federal West chose friends who were similar to themselves in terms of how long they had been at the institution, whether or not they had received major misconduct reports, and whether or not they had been placed in the segregation unit during their stay. Why should we expect these organizational characteristics to be related to friendship choices? These organizational characteristics may actually be related to the interests and values of inmates, which in turn may be directly related to friendship choices. Inmates who entered the institution at the same time will share certain common interests and common problems, which may become the basis for a friendship relationship. The number of misconduct reports and number of times an inmate has been in the segregation unit may be indicative of basic normative orientations which may also constitute the basis for friendship. These characteristics may also constitute indicators of accessibility and proximity. Inmates who entered the institution at the same point in time may more often take part in certain activities together. At Federal East, for instance, all inmates spent a certain amount of time in an Admission and Orientation cottage, where they were housed together with other inmates. A similar, albeit less forceful, argument can be made regarding whether or not an inmate had spent time in the segregation unit. Since the segregation process is less than complete, associations made in the segregation unit may become the bases for friendships.

Length of Stay. The inmates at Federal East were classified into three categories of length of stay: 1-3 months, 4-6 months, and 7-9 months. The inmates at Federal West were classified into four categories: 1-3 months, 4-6 months, 7-12 months, and 13 or more months. Examination of the self-preference ratios of these groups indicated that similarity of length of stay was a relatively important factor affecting friendship choices. The ratios of in-group preference ranged between 3.3 and 3.8 at Federal East, while at Federal West they ranged from 1.7 to 4.2. At both Federal East and Federal West the self-preference ratios were highest for those inmates who had just entered the institutions and those who were closest to leaving the institutions; these are the inmates who we would expect to be most sensitive to the common problems they faced.

Given these data, however, there seems to be little basis for asserting that the relationship between town trip choice and length of stay was stronger at either Federal East or Federal West. On the basis of the observed patterns, we conclude that this relationship was equally strong at both of the institutions.

Number of Major Misconduct Reports. Similarity in terms of whether or not the inmates had received major misconduct reports did not seem to be as important as similarity in terms of length of stay in influencing the town trip choices of the inmates, although similarity in terms of this characteristic may have been more relevant for those inmates who had never received a major misconduct report than for those who had. At both institutions the ratios of self-preference of the "None" groups were closer to two in contrast to the ratios of self-preference of the "One or More" groups whose self-preference ratios more closely approximate unity. It appears that we are encountering a recurrence or a continuation of the pattern we encountered in our review of offense characteristics. The inmates with less serious offense backgrounds tended to choose their own kind, while those with more serious offense backgrounds did not. The tendency of the inmates in the "None" category to choose other inmates of this classification was equally strong at both institutions, and this finding does not lend support to Hypothesis 4c, which posited a stronger relationship at Federal West.

Number of Times in Segregation. A pattern very similar to that discussed above was also discerned in the data regarding whether or not an inmate had ever been in segregation and whether or not his friendship choice had ever been in segregation. Once again we found that the self-preference scores of those respondents classified in the "None" category were greater than those who had been classified as "One or More" in terms of the number of times they had been in segregation. It appeared that those inmates who had never been assigned to the segregation unit were more likely to choose as their town trip choices other inmates who had never been assigned to the segregation unit. On the other hand, those inmates who had been assigned to the segregation unit were less discriminating as to whether or not their town trip choices had been assigned to the segregation unit. This pattern was somewhat more distinct at Federal East than at Federal West.

Friendship Choices and Normative Orientations

Hypothesis 4d *Inmates will tend to be similar to the inmates they choose as friends in terms of their normative orientations.*

There is a fair amount of work in the area of social psychology that suggests that interpersonal attraction and similarity of attitudes are closely related. Hare in his funnel analogy cites common interests or values as the third filter following proximity and similar individual characteristics as the determinants of the friendship process.[12] Lindzey and Byrne have stated that "Perhaps the best documented and most widely studied relationship in the sociometric literature is that between attraction and congruity of attitudes, beliefs, and values."[13] There seems to be little disagreement as to whether there is a significant positive relationship between similarity of attitudes and interpersonal attraction. What debate remains revolves around the theoretical explanation of this relationship. The most important explanations seem to fall into two major categories: those based on a cognitive homeostatis model and those based on reinforcement theory. Festinger, Heider, and Newcomb are the primary proponents of explanations of the first type, while Pepitone and Byrne are proponents of the second type of explanations.[14]

On the basis of this earlier empirical work documenting the relationship between similarity of attitudes and interpersonal attraction we predicted in Hypothesis 4d that there would be a relationship between similarity of normative orientations and friendship choices at the two institutions we are studying. We expected that the inmates would have chosen as friends other inmates who were similar to themselves in terms of the normative orientations as measured by the Conformity Index (presented in Chapter 4). Table 5-3 presents our findings regarding the predicted relationship. At Federal East the ratio of self-preference for the low conformity choosers was 5.8, the self-preference ratios of the medium and high conformity choosers were 1.7. At Federal West only the self-preference ratios of the low conformity groups (2.1) departed from unity. In sum, similarity of conformity orientations did appear to be related to interpersonal attraction at Federal East; it did not appear to be so related for the majority of inmates at Federal West. At both institutions it was the low conformity groups that showed the strongest tendency to make in-group choices.

Why did there exist an almost complete absence of any relationship between the inmate's normative orientation and the normative orientation of his friendship choice at Federal West? Given the restrictive organizational

Table 5-3
Relationship between Town Trip Choice and Conformity Score

Conformity Score of Chooser	Conformity Score of Chosen						Total	Ratio of Self-Preference
	Low		Medium		High			
	O	E	O	E	O	E		
Federal East								
Low	5	1.31	5	5.00	2	5.69	12	5.8
Medium	11	5.77	27	20.51	12	23.72	50	1.7
High	5	6.69	18	24.17	35	27.14	58	1.7
Sum							120	
Federal West								
Low	11	6.36	15	17.95	9	10.69	35	2.1
Medium	15	18.73	51	51.42	35	30.85	101	1.0
High	15	10.76	25	29.74	18	17.51	58	1.0
Sum							194	

climate at Federal West we would have predicted that the extent to which one was willing to conform or refuse to conform to staff norms would have been a much more relevant basis for friendship there than at Federal East. While it is not immediately clear why this relationship should have been weaker at Federal West, some of our earlier findings may throw some light on the situation. One of our findings in Chapter 4 was that a situation of pluralistic ignorance existed to a much greater extent at Federal West than at Federal East. The inmates at Federal West were less able than the inmates at Federal East to estimate the proportion of inmates who were likely to give prosocial responses to the items constituting the conformity index. It is possible that such orientations were seldom if ever discussed by the inmates at Federal West and that the positions of one's friends were assumed to be similar to one's own. The relatively intensive treatment program at Federal East, which utilized group discussion, would have made this situation less likely. One of the important distinctions made in the social psychological literature is that *perceived* similarity of attitudes and interpersonal attraction are related. It may very well be that the perception and the reality were two different things at Federal West.

Summary

An examination of the distribution of Similarity Index scores of friendship and nonfriendship pairings in the living units disclosed that overall similarity on nine variables was related to friendship choice at both institutions. The relationship between similarity and friendship choices was stronger at Federal West as had been hypothesized.

In examining the relationship of each of these variables to friendship choices we found that the friendship choices of the inmates were clearly limited by such factors as proximity and race, factors which have been found to be important determinants of the friendship process outside of the institutions as well. Of greater relevance to our understanding of friendships in institutional settings were the findings regarding offense characteristics, organizational characteristics, and normative orientations. Looking at the overall findings regarding offense and organizational characteristics, one was able to discern what might be described as an emerging pattern: Those inmates who had the less serious offense histories and those inmates who had not gotten into serious trouble in the institution were likely to choose as friends other inmates who were similar to themselves in terms of these characteristics. Those inmates who had more serious offense histories and who had gotten into serious trouble while in the institutions were much less discriminating in their friendship choices, choosing as friends others who were similar and dissimilar to themselves in proportion to their presence in the inmate population. Choice according to similarity in the offense background was more prevalent at Federal West than at Federal East, while choice according to similarity of organizational characteristics was equally relevant at both institutions. Since choices were structured to a certain extent according to similarity of behavior (i.e., past offenses and institutional adjustment), we would expect the friendship choices of the inmates also to be structured in terms of the conformity orientations of the inmates. This was found to be generally true at Federal East but, except for the low conformity inmates, not at Federal West. The one similarity that did exist between Federal East and Federal West on this issue was that at both institutions the self-preference ratios of the low conformity inmates were the highest of the three groups at each institution. This would seem to indicate that those who were most opposed to the staff-endorsed norms of behavior more often stuck together or adapted a mode of solidary opposition vis-a-vis the staff and more conforming inmates. It was suggested that the phenomenon of pluralistic ignorance precluded stronger relationships between the similarity of the inmates' privately held normative orientations and their friendship choices at Federal West. Instead, a relationship may have existed between perceived similarity of normative orientations and friendship choices.

The policy implications of these findings will be addressed in Chapter 7. We now turn to Chapter 6 to an examination of the leadership patterns observed at the two institutions.

Notes

1. Joan H. Criswell, "A Sociometric Study of Race Cleavage in the Classroom," *Archives of Psychology* 33, no. 235 (1939): 1-82; "Sociometric Methods of Measuring Group Preferences," *Sociometry* 7 (1943): 398-408; "Sociometric Measurement and Chance," *Sociometry* 7 (1944): 415-421; "Notes on the Constant Frame of Reference Problem," *Sociometry* 10 (1950): 93-107.

2. A. Paul Hare, *Handbook of Small Group Research* (New York: The Free Press, 1962), p. 139.

3. Gardner Lindzey and Donn Byrne, "Measurement of Social Choice and Interpersonal Attractiveness," in *The Handbook of Social Psychology,* ed. Gardner Lindzey and Elliot Aronson, 2d edition, vol. 2 (Reading, Mass.: Addison-Wesley Publishing Co., 1968), p. 496.

4. Dorothy M. Kipnis, as cited in Lindzey and Byrne, "Measurement of Social Choice," p. 497.

5. Hare, *Handbook of Small Group Research*, p. 140.

6. Lindzey and Byrne, "Measurement of Social Choice," p. 497.

7. Theodore Newcomb, *The Acquaintance Process* (New York: Holt, Rinehart and Winston, 1961), p. 96.

8. Maynard L. Erickson and LaMar T. Empey, "Court Records, Undetected Delinquency and Decision Making," *Journal of Criminal Law, Criminology and Police Science* 54 (1963): 456-469.

9. Martin Gold, *Delinquent Behavior in An American City* (Monterey, Calif.: Brooks Cole Publishing Co., 1970), pp. 32-34.

10. Ibid., p. 92.

11. John Irwin, "The Prison Experience: The Convict World," in *Correctional Institutions*, ed. Robert Carter, Daniel Glaser, and Leslie T. Wilkins, (Philadelphia: J.B. Lippincott Co., 1972), pp. 173-192.

12. Hare, *Handbook of Small Group Research*, p. 140.

13. Lindzey and Byrne, "Measurement of Social Choice," p. 506.

14. Leon Festinger, *A Theory of Cognitive Dissonance* (Stanford: Stanford University Press, 1957); Fritz Heider, *The Psychology of Interpersonal Relations* (New York: Wiley, 1958); Theodore Newcomb, *The Acquaintance Process* (New York: Holt, Rinehart and Winston, 1961); Albert Pepitone, *Attraction and Hostility* (New York: Atherton, 1964); and Donn Byrne, "Attitudes and Attraction" in *Advances in Experimental Social Psychology,* ed. Leonard Berkowitz, vol. 4 (New York: Academic Press, 1969), pp. 36-89.

6

Leadership Patterns: Empirical Findings

In Chapter 6 we continue our consideration of the alternate society by examining the leadership patterns that existed among the inmates at Federal East and Federal West. Who were the inmate leaders at the two institutions? Did the leaders at both institutions possess the same characteristics? On what basis did the inmates identify leaders? How similar to or different from their followers were the leaders identified? These are some of the questions which we hope to answer, as we analyze the data relevant to our fifth set of hypotheses, focusing on leadership patterns within the alternate society.

Leadership in the Prison Setting

It has long been recognized that when a number of individuals interact in the pursuit of common goals or the resolution of common problems, one of the results of such interaction is the emergence of a group structure in which members fulfill different roles and exercise differing degrees of influence. It is to this differential exercise of power that we refer when we write of leadership. It is common to distinguish between influence based on an individual's occupation of a formal office within an organization and influence based on the freely given recognition and consent of one's followers. The former case is generally referred to as authority or headship, the latter as informal leadership. It is the patterns of informal leadership among the inmates that concern us here.

What do we know about the persons who emerge as leaders in various social groups? What makes a leader? One of the things on which students of leadership seem to agree is that it is not possible to come up with a description of the perfect leader for all occasions. Rather, they argue that leadership is the result of the interaction of the personal abilities and characteristics that an individual brings to a situation and the particular demands of the situation itself. Stogdill stated this position as follows:

Theorists no longer explain leadership solely in terms of the individual or the group. Rather, it is believed that characteristics of the individual and the demands of the situation interact in such a manner as to permit one, or perhaps a few, persons to arise to leadership status.[1]

Similarly, Gibb has summarized the relationship between the person and the situation as follows:

Leadership is an interactional phenomenon arising when group formation takes place. The emergence of a group structure, whereby each of its members is assigned a relative position within the group, depending on the nature of his interactional relations with all other members, is a general phenomenon and a function of the interaction of the individuals engaged in the pursuit of a common goal. But the *relative* role an individual member assumes within the group is determined both by the role needs of the group and by the particular attributes of personality, ability, and skill which differentiate him from other members of the group. However (and this is the crux of the interactional theory), "the role he achieves is determined not by his personal qualities in the abstract but by his standing in relation to his fellow members in the *special qualities* required by the particular group goal or situation." (Sherif, 1948: 456)[2]

Different situations will call forth different kinds of persons to be leaders. To the extent that groups face similar kinds of problems, they should have similar kinds of leaders; to the extent that groups face dissimilar problems, they should have dissimilar types of leaders. We have argued that while some similarities existed in the problems faced by the inmates at Federal East and Federal West, dissimilarities also existed. Consequently we would predict that certain kinds of differences should exist in the leadership patterns at the two institutions. Several of our hypotheses directly address this issue. But before examining the data from Federal East and Federal West, let us turn to the question of identifying the inmate leaders and review some of the previous findings on inmate leaders.

A variety of methods have been used to identify leaders in correctional settings, including participant observation, interviews, and survey research questions. Most of the published studies, however, have utilized a version of one of two basic sociometric items, both of which were used in this study. One of these is based on nominations for a hypothetical election to an inmate council. The specific form of this question as used in this study was as follows: "If you had the chance to elect a guy to be part of an advisory council that would discuss things with the director, who would you vote for?" The second kind of question that has been used to identify inmate leaders is a sociometric item, which asks the inmates to identify the inmate who seems to have the most influence in getting others to do what he wants. The specific form of this question which was used in this study was:

Think of the guys you know in your cottage, in school, on work detail or in recreation. Which guy would you say has the most influence among the others here—that is, which guy is best at getting other guys to do what he wants?

Previous studies by Schrag, Grusky, and Berk utilized the first of these two approaches, leadership based on representation nominations.[3] Street utilized the second, leadership based on influence.[4]

In the following analysis we have differentiated between "representation leaders" and "influence leaders" and have designated any inmate who received one or more nominations on the inmate council question as a "representation leader" and any inmate who was named one or more times as being influential as an "influence leader." While the reception of only one nomination may have been a less stringent criterion than we would have liked to have used in identifying the inmate leaders, it seemed to be a reasonable one. The inmates were asked to give only one name in response to each of these two items, and all self-nominations have been removed from the data set. A more stringent definition of leadership would have limited the number of leaders identified so as to rule out the possibility of meaningful comparisons between leaders and nonleaders.

A greater proportion of inmates (24 percent at Federal East and 30 percent at Federal West) were nominated as representation leaders than were named as influence leaders at the two institutions (17 percent and 15 percent at Federal East and Federal West respectively). But perhaps what was most striking was the similarity of the distributions of leadership nominations at the two institutions on both of the leadership measures. The representation leadership choices were somewhat more dispersed at Federal West, where slightly more of the inmates received one or more nominations, but the difference is one of only six percentage points (30 percent at Federal West versus 24 percent at Federal East). On the influence leadership measure the differences between the distributions at the two institutions were even smaller. At Federal East 17 percent of the inmates received one or more nominations; at Federal West 15 percent of the inmates received one or more nominations.

Berk in his study of prison camps found that leadership was more highly concentrated at the custodially oriented camp in contrast to the treatment-oriented camp.[5] In attempting to replicate this finding, Street obtained mixed results, which did not provide clear evidence of such a relationship.[6] Our data provided little indication of differences in the concentration of leadership at Federal East and Federal West.

To what extent were those who were named as representation leaders also named as influence leaders at the two institutions? When we examined the overlap between our two measures of leadership, we could not avoid the conclusion that while there was substantial overlap in terms of the choices received by inmates on our measures of leadership, the groups of individuals identified as influential at the two institutions were not coterminous with the groups of individuals nominated as representation leaders. Approximately half of the inmates who were named as influential at both Federal East and Federal West were also nominated as representation leaders at those institutions. Looking at it somewhat differently, approximately one-third of the inmates who were nominated for the inmate council were also seen as being influential at Federal East; at Federal West approximately one-fourth of those who had been nominated for the inmate council were also seen as being influential. These were the inmates who were seen as being both influential and suitable to represent the other inmates in dealings with the administrations of the institutions. There were also, however, other inmates who were seen as being influential, but who were not nominated for the inmate council, and vice-versa. It appears that our leadership measures were tapping two different functions of leadership and that only a small proportion of the total number of inmates identified on the two measures fulfill both of those functions. We will return to this question later when we discuss the characteristics and orientations of the inmate leaders at Federal East and Federal West.

To what extent were those identified as either influence or representation leaders also well-liked by their fellow inmates? In his study of prison camps, Berk found that in custodially oriented camps, "there tended not only to be fewer leaders, but these leaders were less liked than those in the treatment camp."[7] We have already discussed our finding that there was little difference between the distribution of leadership choices at Federal East and Federal West. To test the applicability of the second part of Berk's statement, we examined the overlap between the persons named as leaders and the persons named as friends on the friendship measure presented in Chapter 5. We indeed found a good deal of overlap between our two measures of leadership and our friendship measure. At both institutions the vast majority of those who were named as leaders were also chosen by other inmates as town trip partners. We also found, however, that the leaders at Federal West were slightly more popular than the leaders at Federal East. Ninety-one percent of the influence leaders at Federal West had also been named as town trip choices by at least one inmate, in comparison to 83 percent of the influence leaders at Federal East. Similarly 94 percent of the representation leaders at Federal West were named as friends, while only 86 percent of the Federal East representation leaders were named as friends. While the percentage differences were not large, they were clearly in the opposite direction from those found by Berk.

The findings are, however, congruent with the previous findings of Grusky who found that, in general, "the informal leaders tend to choose more friends, be chosen more themselves, and are more likely to be involved in mutual choice friendship cliques than are the nonleaders."[8]

Characteristics of the Inmate Leaders

In Chapter 2 we presented a number of hypotheses regarding factors we would expect, on the basis of previous research and our model of the alternate society, to be related to leadership in correctional institutions. These factors were length of stay, age, education, and offense history. We examined the distribution of leaders and nonleaders on each of these variables. As explained above, we dichotomized leadership status into two categories, leader and nonleader. Similarly, we dichotomized the variables of length of stay, age, education, type of offense, and number of previous offenses into two categories. Yule's Q, a special case of gamma appropriate for use with two-by-two tables, was chosen as the measure of association. The categories used in the analysis and the obtained Q scores are presented in Table 6-1. The most significant finding in this table is not one or more of the individual relationships reported, but rather the overall patterning evident among those relationships.

Length of Stay and Leadership Status.

Hypothesis 5a *Leadership status will be related to length of stay in the institution. Leaders will have been in the institution longer than nonleaders.*

Overall, we found moderate support for Hypothesis 5a. In three of the four relationships examined for this variable, leadership status was associated with a longer length of stay. How does one explain the deviant

Table 6-1
Summary of Relationships Found between Leadership Status and Characteristics
(Q scores)

	Representation Leadership		Influence Leadership	
	Federal East	*Federal West*	*Federal East*	*Federal West*
Hypothesis				
5a *Length of Stay* 6 months or less More than 6 mos.	+.24	+.06	+.25	+.26
5b *Age* 19 and under 20 and over	+.48	+.20	+.30	+.30
5c *Education* 9th grade or less 10th grade or more	+.39	+.13	+.06	+.08
5d *Offense History* 1. Type of Offense Public Order/Property Person-Oriented	−.09	−.20	−.16	+.11
2. Number of Previous Offenses 3 or less 4 or more	−.18	.00	+.22	+.18

case—the lack of a relationship between representation leadership and length of stay at Federal West? One explanation is that the qualities needed to serve in a liaison function with the administration of the institution do not include a certain amount of seniority at Federal West. We have previously presented evidence that in general the inmates at Federal West were more negative and less conforming than the inmates at Federal East. It may be that the Federal West inmates, in choosing representatives to meet with the administration, chose other inmates who had not been around long enough to have established bad reputations in the eyes of the staff. Since the inmate culture at Federal East was not as negatively oriented and since seniority in the institution received indirect recognition and status through the system of "class levels," the inmates who had been at the institution would be the ones more likely to be selected. As for the other relationships found between leadership status and length of stay, we would argue that the explanation we offered earlier—that a certain amount of time is needed to get to know the system and to get to be known—is appropriate and adequate.

In sum, there was a moderate positive relationship between influence leadership and length of stay, but the relationship between representation leadership and length of stay appears to vary with organizational climate.

Age and Leadership Status.

Hypothesis 5b *Age will be related to leadership status in juvenile and youth institutions. Leaders in general will be older than nonleaders.*

The evidence in support of Hypothesis 5b was both somewhat stronger and more consistent than that found for leadership and length of stay above. The associations found were all positive and of at least moderate strength ranging from $+.20$ to $+.48$. Here once again, however, we find that organizational climate has some apparent impact on the relationship of our independent variable (age in this instance) and representation leadership status. The inmates at Federal East were much more likely to choose older inmates to represent them on an inmate council than the inmates at Federal West.

Education and Leadership Status.

Hypothesis 5c *In general, inmate leaders will have more education than nonleaders.*

With the exception of the association between representation leadership and education at Federal East ($Q = +.39$), the associations between leadership status and education, while positive, were generally of negligible strength. Here again, however, we find the strongest association for representation leaders at Federal East, much as we have observed for the preceding variables of age and length of stay. Given that this association was found for the representation leaders, one must question whether this indicates that education per se was facilitative of leadership or whether it was a reflection of what the inmates thought the staff would expect in inmate representatives.

Offense History and Leadership Status.

Hypothesis 5d *Inmate leaders will have more serious offense histories in terms of the types and numbers of offenses than will nonleaders.*

The relationship between leadership status and offense history is the most complex of those examined. There seems to have been a negligible to low negative association between having committed a person-oriented offense and leadership, except for the influence leaders at Federal West, where there was a low positive association.

The association between number of previous offenses and representation leadership was a low negative one at Federal East; there was no relationship between these variables at Federal West. The situation changed somewhat when we looked at influence leadership and number of previous offenses. Here we found a moderate positive association ($Q = +.22$) at Federal East and a low positive association ($Q = +.18$) at Federal West.

How can we explain a negative association or a complete absence of an association between number of previous offenses and representation leadership and positive association between number of previous offenses and influence leadership at the two institutions? One possible explanation is that the inmates in choosing representation leaders chose, consciously or unconsciously, inmates who would be acceptable to or have clout with the staff, i.e., inmates with backgrounds more acceptable to the staff. This group was not identical to the group that actually had influence among the inmates. It appears that there were two groups of "leaders": one which was seen as qualified to serve in a liaison role with the staff and another that actually wielded influence among the inmates themselves. As we have suggested earlier, there was overlap between the two groups, but they were not identical. As we have seen with our hypothesis relating number of offenses to leadership status, whether or not one's predictions are confirmed may depend on the leadership measure used and the type of leaders identified.

Orientations of Inmate Leaders

Hypothesis 5e *Relatively uncooperative and negative leaders will emerge in the inmate groups found in restrictive organizational climates; relatively cooperative and positive leaders will emerge in the inmate groups found in permissive organizational climates.*

We argued in Chapter 2 that one of the consequences of a restrictive organizational climate was the emergence of uncooperative and negative leaders. The unfavorable balance of gratifications and deprivations, the requirements of social control, and the social distance between inmates facilitate the emergence of inmate leaders who are willing to challenge the staff and rules of the institution. On the other hand, the favorable balance of gratification and deprivations, the relative freedom, and the lack of social distance at institutions with what we have called permissive organizational climates will all favor the emergence of cooperative and positive leaders. Berk in his comparative study of prison camps saw leaders emerging to fulfill different functions at different kinds of camps. The main function of leaders in a restrictive organizational climate was that of control, while the main function of inmate leaders in a permissive organizational setting was that of integration and coordination.[9] Both Berk and Street found that the inmate leaders in institutions characterized by what we have termed permissive organizational climates maintained more positive attitudes toward the institutions, their staffs, and the programs than did nonleaders. In the institutions with restrictive organizational climates the leaders tended to be more negative than the nonleaders.[10] Table 6-2 presents our findings on the orientations of the inmate leaders at Federal East and Federal West using the conformity index presented previously as our operational measure of the inmates' orientations.

There was a moderate positive association between prosocial conformity orientations and representation leadership at Federal East, with a gamma of +.28. The association, while still positive, was considerably smaller at Federal West, where the gamma score obtained was +.06. Looking at our second measure of leadership, which was based on the exercise of influence among the inmates themselves, we find a moderate negative relationship between this measure and conformity at Federal East ($\gamma = -.22$) and negligible negative association ($\gamma = -.08$) at Federal West. With a change in leadership measures there also came a change in the direction of the association: representation leadership was positively associated with conformity, while influence leadership was negatively associated with conformity orientations. The associations for both kinds of leadership were stronger at Federal East than at Federal West. Perhaps the most significant conclusion to be derived from this analysis and that of the tables immediately

Table 6-2
Leadership and Conformity Orientations
(percentages)

Conformity Score	Representation Leadership			
	Federal East		Federal West	
	Nonleaders	Leaders	Nonleaders	Leaders
Low	12	8	20	16
Medium	44	32	50	53
High	44	60	30	31
	(120)	(37)	(199)	(77)
	$\gamma = +.28$		$\gamma = +.06$	

Conformity Score	Influence Leadership			
	Federal East		Federal West	
	Nonleaders	Leaders	Nonleaders	Leaders
Low	11	17	18	24
Medium	41	45	51	47
High	48	38	31	29
	(133)	(24)	(242)	(34)
	$\gamma = -.22$		$\gamma = -.08$	

preceding is that the relationship between orientations and leadership depends heavily on both the kind of leadership identified and the organizational setting. This conclusion does not clearly support our original hypothesis regarding the importance of organizational settings. It does, however, emphasize the need to differentiate among the operational measures of leadership used when comparing other research studies. It is becoming increasingly clear that the inmates themselves differentiated the kinds of inmates who fulfilled different leadership functions.

An alternate way of attempting to answer the question of what kinds of leaders predominated at the two institutions was to ask the inmates themselves. Table 6-3 presents the inmates' perceptions of the leaders at Federal East and Federal West. On all the four questions asked of the inmates about leaders, the Federal East inmates gave much more positive responses. The differences in responses to these items at the two institutions were substantial: only on the fourth item in Table 6-3 was the difference between the responses at Federal East and Federal West less than 20 percentage points. The Federal East inmates saw the inmate leaders as being much more cooperative and reform-oriented than did the Federal West inmates.

Table 6-3
Inmates' Perceptions of Leaders
(percentages)

	Federal East	Federal West
Agree that:		
Most of the leaders are ready to fight other guys at most any time.	44	73
Most of the leaders will have little or nothing to do with the staff.	28	58
Most of the leaders are trying to straighten out and make the most of their stay.	69	49
Most of the leaders are the guys who are best at "conning" the staff.	42	49
	(170-173)	(288-299)

Leaders and Their Followers: Personal, Offense,
and Organizational Similarities

Hypothesis 5f *Inmates will tend to choose as leaders other inmates who are similar to themselves in terms of various personal, offense, and organizational characteristics.*

Hypothesis 5g *Inmates will tend to limit their choices of leaders to inmates who are similar to themselves in terms of personal, offense, and organizational characteristics more often in restrictive organizational climates than in permissive organizational climates.*

We will consider these two hypotheses simultaneously, just as we considered Hypotheses 4b and 4c, which dealt with the personal, offense, and organizational similarities between friends. Again, we have used the following empirical indicators of these conceptual categories:

Personal Characteristics
  Age
  Race
  Social Class

Offense Characteristics
  Number of Previous Offenses
  Type of Offense
  Previous Institutionalization

Organizational Characteristics
   Length of Stay
   Number of Major Misconduct Reports
   Number of Times in Segregation

Since Hypotheses 5f and 5g, and 5h that follows, deal with the leaders *chosen* by the inmates, we have utilized only our measure of representation leadership in examining these hypotheses.

We expected the inmates to choose as representation leaders other inmates who were similar to themselves for basically the same reasons they chose friends who were similar to themselves. In many cases they will choose leaders from among their friends. In those cases where the leaders they select are not from among their friends, they will select others similar to themselves on the premise that similarity in terms of these characteristics will be related to similarity of values and interests.

Previous empirical evidence for Hypothesis 5f can be found in the earlier work of Schrag, one of the few researchers to address directly this question in a correctional setting. Schrag found that inmates tended to select as leaders other inmates who were similar to themselves in terms of ethnic background, intelligence, number of previous offenses, nature of offense, length of sentences, institutional adjustment, and pathological and psychological diagnoses. On the other hand, similarity in terms of age, occupation, education, or marital status was not related to the inmates' choices of leaders.[11]

Our rationale for Hypothesis 5g flows from our more general argument regarding the nature of the alternate society in permissive and restrictive organizational climates. Just as we have argued that there would be greater closure of friendship choices on the basis of external or categorical characteristics in restrictive organizational climates, we also believed that a similar type of closure would be evident in the inmates' selection of leaders.

Paralleling the approach we took in Chapter 5 we will utilize the Similarity Index, which was introduced there to determine the degree of overall similarity that existed between the inmates and the representation leaders they chose on the nine variables cited. We will compare the distribution of these scores with the distribution of similarity scores between our respondents and those in their living units whom they did not select as leaders. We also will utilize again Criswell's self-preference ratio to determine the extent to which inmates chose as leaders other inmates who were similar to themselves on each of the nine variables separately.

Overall Similarity. The Similarity Index that was introduced in Chapter 5 to determine the degree of similarity that existed among friends was used to determine the degree of similarity that existed between the inmates and the representation leaders they nominated. Comparisons were made for pairings within living units, and the results were then summed across living units to obtain the overall distributions for the institutions. A pair of inmates were considered very similar if the index score for the pairing was 5 or greater. Table 6-4 presents the distributions of follower-leader pairings and follower-nonleader pairings found at the two institutions.

According to the data presented in Table 6-4 the inmates at Federal East did not overselect as leaders those inmates who were most similar to themselves. As a matter of fact, a greater proportion of the inmates who were not named as leaders were very similar to the respondent inmates in contrast to those actually named as leaders. At Federal West, however, we found that similarity was related to the selection of leaders. There 63 percent of the follower-leader pairs were classified as very similar while only 42 percent of the possible pairings of the respondents with those they did not choose as leaders were classified as very similar.

On the basis of the distribution of our Similarity Index scores we conclude that similarity was related to the selection of leaders at Federal West but not at Federal East, and, as a corollary, that the tendency for inmates to choose as leaders other inmates similar to themselves was stronger at Federal West.

Age. In the earlier part of this chapter we determined that there was a positive association between leadership status and age at the two institutions. Was this association due to the tendency of older inmates to select only older inmates as leaders, or was it due to a tendency on the part of all inmates to select older inmates as leaders?

Table 6-4
Distribution of Very Similar Pairs among Leader and Nonleader Choices
(percentages)

	Between Choosers and Leaders Chosen	Between Choosers and Nonleaders [a]
Federal East	58	63
	(62)[b]	(1994)[c]
Federal West	63	42
	(65)[b]	(3771)[c]

[a]Nonleaders are all the other inmates in the living units for whom the full complement of data was available.

[b]This is the number of within-living-unit follower-leader pairs for which similarity index scores were available in the institution.

[c]This is the number of possible within-living-unit pairings of choosers with those they did not choose as a leader and for whom similarity index scores were available within the institution.

The ratios of self-preference obtained indicated that the younger inmates tended to underselect other inmates of their own age as leaders and like the older inmates tended to overselect older inmates as leaders. The self-preference ratios of the inmates nineteen and below failed to achieve unity at either institution; the self-preference ratios of the inmates twenty and above equaled or exceeded a factor of three at both institutions. While the younger inmates at Federal West were less likely to select older leaders than their Federal East counterparts, the younger and older inmates at both sites tended to overselect older inmates. These findings differ from those of Schrag, cited above, regarding the significance of age. We would attribute the difference to the differences in the age ranges of the inmates studied. Schrag studied an adult offender population; our subject population consists of young men in their mid to late adolescence, when several years of age and experience can be much more meaningful.

Race. Schrag had found that similarity in terms of racial background was a very important factor in the inmates' leadership choices.[12] Our examination of friendship choices in the previous chapter also highlighted the importance of racial similarity. Examination of the self-preference ratios indicated that racial similarity was also important in the selection of inmate leaders. The self-preference scores for all categories indicate that the inmates tended to overselect inmates of the same race. The group exhibiting the greatest closure was that of the black inmates at Federal West (self-preference ratio = 26.1), the group exhibiting the least closure was the white inmates at Federal East (self-preference ratio = 1.5). We had previously found a complete lack of friendship ties between blacks and Indians at Federal West; here we found almost a perfect replication of that absence of ties. The black inmates named no Indian inmates as council representatives; on the basis of chance they should have selected at least three. The Indians did name one black as a choice for the inmate council; according to our chance model they, too, should have selected at least three. The self-preference ratios at Federal West exceeded those at Federal East in all instances, lending support to Hypothesis 5g, which predicted greater closure at Federal West.

Social Class. The ratios of self-preference on the basis of social class ranged from 1.2 to 2.3 at the two institutions, with the exception of the lower-class inmates at Federal East, who had a self-preference ratio of .4, indicating that they chose other inmates of their own social class as leaders less than half as often as we would have expected them to on the basis of their numbers in the inmate population. The tendency to choose as leaders other inmates who were similar to themselves in terms of social class was greatest for the upper class inmates at Federal West (self-preference ratio = 2.3).

However, given the moderate level of the self-preference ratios and the overall distribution of observed and expected choices, we cannot conclude that social class similarity was an important factor in the inmates' choices of representation leaders. This conclusion is consistent with the findings of Schrag if we accept his measure of occupation as an indicator of social class status.[13] We do note, however, that in relation to Hypothesis 5g, the self-preference ratios of the inmates at Federal West exceeded those of their counterparts at Federal East in two out of three instances.

Number of Previous Offenses. Schrag had found that inmates tended to choose as leaders other inmates who had committed a similar number of previous offenses.[14] We found that this was true only of those inmates at Federal East and Federal West who were recorded as having no previous offenses. The inmates at Federal East who were recorded as having no previous offenses had a self-preference ratio of 2.8; their Federal West counterparts had a self-preference ratio of 4.0. Some caution must be used in interpreting these results because of the extremely small number of inmates in this category: fifteen at Federal East and sixteen at Federal West. However, an examination of the choices of the other inmates at both institutions indicated that they tended to underselect others who were similar to themselves and to overselect inmates who were recorded as having no previous offenses. This finding is further confirmation of our argument that the inmates selected as representation leaders other inmates who had characteristics that would cause them to be viewed favorably by the administration of the institution. To the extent that the inmates did tend to choose others similar to themselves, that tendency was slightly greater at Federal West than at Federal East. In two out of three instances, the Federal West inmates had higher self-preference ratios.

Type of Offense. On the basis of our previous arguments regarding similarity and Schrag's findings[15] we expected the inmates to choose as leaders other inmates who had committed offenses of the same general nature that they themselves had. This was true of the Public Order offenders at both institutions, and, to a lesser degree, of the Person-Oriented offenders at Federal West.

The Public Order offenders tended to overselect other Public Order offenders as representation leaders at both institutions approximately eleven times more often than would be expected on the basis of their proportions in the inmate groups. The Person-Oriented offenders at Federal West selected other Person-Oriented offenders two and a half times as often as would be expected on the basis of chance. (We did not examine the leadership choice of the Person-Oriented offenders at Federal East because of their very small number.) The Property offenders, who constituted the majority of inmates at both Federal East and Federal West, tended to underselect each other and to overselect Public Order offenders as representation leaders. The ratios of self-preference tended to be somewhat higher at Federal West than at Federal East.

Previous Institutionalization. While we know of no direct evidence to predict that inmates would choose other inmates who were similar to themselves in terms of previous institutional experience, given the findings regarding the relevance of the number of previous offenses and the type of offense for leadership choices, we would predict that similarity in terms of previous institutional experience would be a significant factor. The data indicated that our prediction did not hold. There was a slight tendency for all inmates at Federal East to select as leaders inmates without previous institutional experience. There was also a slight tendency for the inmates without institutional experience at both institutions to overselect others similar to themselves. At Federal East the self-preference ratio for those with no previous institutionalization was 1.6; at Federal West it was 1.2. Given the magnitude of the ratios of self-preference, we must conclude that there was no evidence of a relationship between the previous institutional experience of followers and leaders. It is also impossible to say at which institution the tendency to choose a leader from within one's own classification was stronger.

Length of Stay. Why might we expect inmates to choose as leaders other inmates who have been in the institution the same amount of time as they themselves have? Generally, we would expect that length of stay would be related to the specific interests and concerns of the inmates and that the inmates in choosing a representative for an inmate council would choose someone who shared those interests and concerns. We have already found in the previous chapter that inmates tended to choose as friends inmates who had been in the institution a similar length of time. For these reasons we would expect there to be a positive relationship between the length of stay of followers and the length of stay of their leaders.

Only for the inmates with the longest lengths of stay at the two institutions did the self-preference ratios substantially depart from unity. The inmates at Federal East who had been at the institution for more than seven months chose leaders from their own ranks more than 7.5 times as often as would have been expected on the basis of chance. The self-preference ratio for the inmates at Federal West who had been in the institution the longest, thirteen months or more, was 3.2. The general pattern at both Federal East and Federal West was one of the inmates slightly overselecting other inmates who had been in the institution for approximately the same or a greater length of time as themselves. At both institutions the highest ratios of self-preference were those of the inmates who had been there the longest. The inmates who had seniority tended to limit their leadership choices to others with an equal amount of seniority. This tendency of the senior inmates was stronger at Federal East than at Federal West. It is difficult to generalize about the relative strength of this tendency among the other groups of inmates at the two institutions.

Number of Major Misconduct Reports. Schrag had found that inmates chose as leaders other inmates whose records of institutional adjustment were similar to their own.[16] We have employed two empirical indicators for the purposes of our analysis here: number of major misconduct reports and number of times in segregation.

Although all the ratios of self-preference of those who had no misconduct reports and those who had one or more misconduct reports in their files exceeded unity as we had predicted, none was greater than 1.5. The evidence, while consistent with our hypothesis, cannot be considered conclusive. Nor was it possible to say that there was more in-group closure at one institution than at the other.

Number of Times in Segregation. Our second indicator of institutional adjustment was the number of times the inmate had been placed in segregation. The data provided a somewhat mixed picture. The inmates at Federal East and Federal West who had not been in the segration unit tended to slightly overselect inmates who were similar to themselves, the self-preference ratios being 1.4 and 1.3 respectively. While the small number (14) of inmates at Federal East who had been in segregation one or more times requires a cautious conclusion, their self-preference ratio of .3 certainly justifies the statement that they did not tend to overselect similar inmates. It did appear, however, that the inmates at Federal West who had been in segregation one or more times did tend to overselect other inmates as leaders (self-preference ratio = 1.8) who were similar to themselves in this regard.

Leaders and Their Followers:
Normative Orientations

Hypothesis 5h *Inmates will tend to choose as leaders other inmates who hold normative orientations similar to their own.*

One of the criteria we would expect the inmates to employ in selecting inmate leaders to represent them is a similarity of viewpoint. We would predict that inmates would choose other inmates who share their own value orientations and who could be counted on to react to the administration of the institution in the same manner the inmates themselves would. We have, therefore, hypothesized that conformity orientations of the leaders would be similar to those of the inmates who named them as leaders. Table 6-5 presents our findings relevant to this question. The data presented here do not support our hypothesis. While there was a tendency for the inmates in the low conformity categories at both institutions to overselect leaders with orientations similar to their own, a pattern we earlier observed in our examination of friendship choices, the very small total number of inmates in these categories precludes us from reaching any strong conclusions on the basis of these data. Overall, the observed distribution of leadership choices is very similar to that expected on the basis of chance.

It was reasonable to predict that inmates would use similarity of normative orientations as a criterion in choosing leaders, yet we found little evidence that this was actually the case. In Chapter 5 we found weaker and less uniform relationships between friendship choices and similarity of orientations than we expected. We suggested that the phenomenon of pluralistic ignorance may have been operative there. If this was indeed the case, it is very likely that our lack of relationship between leadership choice and similarity of orientations may be attributed to the same phenomenon.

Table 6-5
Relationship between Conformity Scores of Representation Leaders and Conformity Scores of Followers

| Conformity Scores of Followers | Conformity Scores of Leaders | | | | | | Total | Ratio of Self-Preference |
| | Low | | Medium | | High | | | |
	O	E	O	E	O	E		
Federal East								
Low	1	0.69	4	2.48	1	2.83	6	1.5
Medium	4	2.53	9	9.11	9	10.36	22	1.0
High	2	4.83	18	17.39	22	19.78	42	1.2
Sum							70	
Federal West								
Low	5	3.44	9	9.71	5	5.78	19	1.6
Medium	5	9.59	27	27.08	21	16.11	53	1.0
High	8	5.79	16	16.35	8	9.73	32	0.8
Sum							104	

Summary

The overall distribution of leadership choices at the two institutions tended to be very similar: there did not appear to be any major differences in the concentration of leadership patterns at Federal East and Federal West.

Possibly one of the more significant findings of this chapter was that while there was significant overlap between the group of inmates we have identified as representation leaders and the group we have identified as influence leaders, they were by no means identical. Whether or not we found support or disconfirming evidence for some of our predictions depended in some instances on the measure of leadership chosen. In some cases the strength of the relationship varied with the leadership measure used; in others the direction of the association was reversed. For instance, if we look at the relationship between the inmate's number of previous offenses and whether or not he was selected as a representation leader, we find a Q of $-.18$ at Federal East and no relationship whatsoever at Federal West. Looking at the relationship between number of previous offenses and influence leadership status, on the other hand, we found a positive association: $Q = +.22$ at Federal East and $Q = +.18$ at Federal West. A similar type of reversal also took place when we examined the relationship between the inmate's conformity orientation and leadership status. In general, there was a tendency for the inmates to select as representation leaders those inmates who possessed characteristics that were likely to be approved by staff, while the inmates who were named as influence leaders more often had characteristics that would be likely to be viewed in a less favorable manner. The inmates appeared to be making a distinction between a cadre of leaders who were best suited to represent them to the staff, and a cadre of leaders who actually exerted influence over other inmates (but who would not be as well-suited to represent them in discussions and negotiations with staff). Which of these cadres we identified as the leaders in the institution had important consequences for our findings.

Except in the case of the relationship between type of offense and leadership status, the direction of the association between various personal, offense, and organizational characteristics and leadership status was generally the same at the two institutions, although in most instances the relationships tended to be stronger at Federal East than at Federal West. Overall, we would conclude that the relationships between background characteristics and leadership status tended to be weak to moderate in strength, varied significantly according to the leadership measure employed, and varied, to a lesser extent, from institution to institution. At Federal East representation leaders were more likely than nonleaders to have high conformity scores; influence leaders were more likely than nonleaders to have low conformity scores. At Federal West there was little if any association between leadership status on either measure and conformity score. The inmates' perceptions of their leaders were much more favorable at Federal East than at Federal West.

Similarity Index scores indicated that at Federal West overall similarity was related almost as strongly to leadership selections as it had been to friendship choices. This was not the case at Federal East, however. There the other inmates tended to be slightly more similar to our inmate respondents than the inmates selected as leaders by those respondents. This finding again emphasized the interrelationship of the organizational climate and the nature of the alternate society.

Similarity in terms of race was an important factor in the selection of leaders for all racial groups at both institutions. To a lesser extent, length of stay was also relevant in that the inmates at both institutions who had longer lengths of stay tended to overchoose other inmates who had longer lengths of stay. Self-preference patterns were also evident in the leadership choices of certain subgroups of inmates at Federal West but not at Federal East: inmates who had been in segregation one or more times, who had committed crimes against persons, and who were of middle- or upper-class background. Inmates at both institutions did tend to overselect as leaders certain types of inmates who were not necessarily similar to themselves: older inmates, inmates with few offenses, and inmates who had committed public order types of offenses tended to be overchosen by all inmates at both institutions. Similarity in terms of normative orientations appeared to have almost no relationship to the inmates' leadership choices, a condition that we suggested was due to the pluralistic ignorance that characterizes the inmate subculture.

Notes

1. Ralph M. Stogdill, *Handbook of Leadership; A Survey of Theory and Leadership* (New York: The Free Press, 1974), p. 23.

2. Cecil A. Gibb, "Leadership," in *The Handbook of Social Psychology*, ed. Gardner Lindzey and Elliot Aronson, vol. 4, (Reading, Mass.: Addison-Wesley Publishing Co., 1969), p. 268.

3. Clarence Schrag, "Leadership among Prison Inmates," *American Sociological Review* 19 (1954): 37-42; Oscar Grusky, "Treatment Goals and Organizational Behavior: A Study of an Experimental Prison Camp" (Ph.D. dissertation, University of Michigan, 1957); and Bernard Berk, "Informal Social Organization and Leadership among Inmates in Treatment and Custodial Prisons: A Comparative Study" (Ph.D. dissertation, University of Michigan, 1961).

4. David Street, "Inmate Social Organization: A Comparative Study of Juvenile Correctional Institutions" (Ph.D. dissertation, University of Michigan, 1962).

5. Berk, "Informal Social Organization and Leadership," p. 116.

6. Street, "Inmate Social Organization," p. 178.

7. Berk, "Informal Social Organization and Leadership," p. 145.

8. Grusky, "Treatment Goals and Organizational Behavior," p. 175.

9. Berk, "Informal Social Organization and Leadership," pp. 113-116.

10. Ibid., pp. 122-129; and Street, "Inmate Social Organization," pp. 112-119.

11. Schrag, "Leadership among Prison Inmates," p. 41.

12. Ibid.

13. Ibid.

14. Ibid.

15. Ibid.

16. Ibid.

7 Summary and Conclusions

We began this treatise with "some musings on a grim tale," reviewing Clemmer's original formulation of the prisonization hypothesis and the later research, which pointed to the necessity of qualifying Clemmer's original formulation. We found it necessary to qualify the prisonization hypothesis to take account of the values and orientations which the inmates bring with them into the institution, differences in the gratifications and deprivations present in different institutions, and the changing nature of institutions. We reviewed a number of different conceptualizations of the inmate subculture and proposed that it could be more fruitfully conceptualized as an "alternate society," an alternate social structure through which the inmate occupants seek to meet their physical, psychological, and social needs that have not been met by the formal structure of the correctional institution. It was further proposed that the extent to which the values and norms of the alternate society were congruent or incongruent with those of the larger society outside of the institution was an empirical question. Previous explanations of the inmate subculture have tended to fall into one of two basic categories: explanations based on a deprivation model or explanations based on an importation model. The task of this research was seen not as the determination as to which of these models was the correct one but rather as that of attempting to determine the relative contribution of each to our understanding of the alternate society. It was hypothesized, however, that the deprivation model would be the more useful of the two in explaining the normative content of the alternate society.

The concept of organizational climates was explicated in the context of the deprivation model, and two ideal types of organizational climates were delineated: the permissive and the restrictive. An examination of the two research sites indicated that the organizational climate at Federal East was considerably more permissive than the organizational climate that prevailed at Federal West, although the conditions at neither institution approached the polar extremes. The significance of the inmates' background characteristics was discussed in the context of the importation model of prisonization, and it was found that while the inmates at the two institutions were very similar in most respects, there were differences on several variables that have special significance within the importation model. The inmates at Federal West had committed more numerous and more serious offenses than had the inmates at Federal East.

119

Having formulated our research task and having described our research populations in the terms of our theoretical framework, we proceeded to examine empirically five sets of hypotheses regarding prisonization and social relationships within the inmate groups at the two Federal correctional institutions for young offenders.

Findings and Implications

Major Variables Affecting the Alternate Society

We had predicted that inmates in institutions with permissive organizational climates would be more likely to manifest a commitment to nonprisonized adaptations than would inmates in institutions with restrictive climates. Our initial analysis focused only on organizational climates, and the responses of the inmates supported this prediction. We went on to predict that the background characteristics of the inmates would also have an impact on their adaptations to the institutional experience. In examining the relationship between inmate responses and various personal, offense, and organizationally assigned characteristics, we found moderately strong negative relationships between inmate conformity responses and number of previous offenses, length of stay, number of major misconduct reports, and the number of times an inmate had been in the segregation unit. The relationships between the inmates' orientations and length of stay was consistent with the deprivation model of prisonization for which we had already found some support. On the other hand, the negative relationship between prosocial conformity orientations and the number of previous offenses the inmates had committed provided support for the importation model of prisonization. On further examination we found that organizational climate and background characteristics (number of previous offenses) appeared to have additive effects on the orientations of the inmates: the inmates at Federal East with the lesser number of previous offenses had the highest prosocial conformity scores, while the inmates at Federal West with the greater number of previous offenses had the lowest prosocial conformity scores.

We had predicted that organizational climate would have a greater impact on the inmate orientations than would background characteristics. We found that this was the case for those inmates who had committed three or fewer previous offenses. For those inmates who had committed four or more offenses, differences in organizational climate had but a negligible association with the conformity orientations of the inmates.

If we accept our measure of conformity orientations as an indicator of the extent to which the inmates shared certain values with staff and were willing to cooperate with staff, these findings have important implications for correctional policy. Of the inmates who had committed less than three previous offenses, those who were in a restrictive organizational climate were much less likely to express prosocial conformity orientations. While we have not completely ruled out other explanations, this evidence is certainly consistent with the deprivation model argument that inmate orientations are influenced by the organizational setting. By placing inmates who are not yet deeply committed to a life of crime (as indicated by the number of offenses they have committed) in a restrictive organizational climate, we are in effect facilitating the "prisonization" process and perhaps even wasting the potential for rehabilitation that may be present. If nothing else, these findings clearly indicate that first offenders or offenders who do not have extensive records should be placed in relatively permissive settings rather than in restrictive settings. To do otherwise is to stack the deck against our own efforts at reform. Conversely, the data also indicate that in the case of those offenders who have been extensively involved in violating the law, minor differences in organizational settings may not make that much difference to their willingness to cooperate with staff.

Integration within the Alternate Society

It was hypothesized that inmates in permissive organizational climates would display more highly developed patterns of integration than would inmates in restrictive organizational climates. We found that while intensity of association was greater at Federal West than at Federal East, the extensiveness of contacts was greater, and the inmates more positively valued their associations at Federal East. Utilizing a composite measure, which combined measures of intensiveness, extensiveness, and evaluation of acquaintances, we found a low negative association between integration and a restrictive organizational climate, a finding consistent with our hypothesis.

It was also predicted that voluntary interaction among inmates would vary directly with the amount of interaction between staff and inmates. While we did not have a direct measure of the amount of staff-inmate and inmate-inmate interaction, we did find that at Federal East there was a positive association between the inmates' perception of accessibility of staff and their integration scores; at Federal West there was a negative association between these variables. We see this as providing partial confirmation of the hypothesis, while indicating the need to note the differential impact of organizational climates.

In examining the relationship between length of stay in the institution and integration, we found no evidence of the previously reported inverse U-shaped relationship. What differences existed between the two institutions were probably due to the different organizational policies governing the placement of new inmates within the inmate population.

Previous research had led us to believe that integration among the inmates would vary inversely with the heterogeneity of the inmate group, and our finding of a greater degree of integration at Federal East where the inmate group was less heterogeneous than at Federal West is consistent with that statement.

Although a majority of the inmates had been previously institutionalized, we were not able to detect any relationships between previous institutionalization and integration at either of the two institutions.

We found no relationship whatsoever between age and integration at Federal East, but there was a low negative association between age and integration at Federal West.

On the basis of previous research we had predicted inverse relationships between integration and extrainstitutional ties; what we found were direct relationships at both institutions (moderate in strength at Federal East and low in strength at Federal West). Further analysis indicated an even stronger relationship between frequency of contact with parents and extensiveness of friendships within the institutions. One explanation for this relationship was based on the fact that the inmates were still basically adolescents, participating in an adolescent peer group while still maintaining ties to their parents.

In sum, the findings just reviewed indicate that certain organizational arrangements did have an impact on and were reflected in the social structure of the inmate groups, as we had predicted. However, the statistical findings actually portray a rather colorless portrait of the differences that existed in the relationships among the inmates in contrast to our on-the-site observations. To merely say that there was slightly less integration at Federal West than at Federal East fails to capture the loneliness and fear of the inmates at Federal West who reported instances of "skull-dragging" or of the inmate who described his choices of "fuck, fight, or hit the fence." While the statistical differences between Federal East and Federal West were not great on our measures of integration, they were consistent with our predictions regarding integration and organizational climate and together with our observational data lend support to our argument that those conditions we have described as constituting a permissive organizational climate facilitate relationships among the inmates that are primarily supportive and expressive rather than parasitical and instrumental. If, indeed, the purpose of our correctional institutions is to resocialize and prepare offenders, especially young offenders, for reentry into society, our goals ought to be to provide the offender as inmate with the types of social relationships we would like to see the offender as citizen maintain outside the institution.

Integration and Inmate Attitudes

We had predicted that integration would be positively associated with pro-social conformity orientations at Federal East and negatively associated with prosocial conformity orientations at Federal West. We found instead that there was a low negative relationship between integration and prosocial conformity responses at both institutions. Outside contacts were, however, related positively to both integration scores and prosocial conformity scores. Further analysis revealed that the relationships among these variables were very different at the two institutions. At Federal East it was among the inmates who had the most outside contacts that there was a moderate negative relationship between integration and conformity; at Federal West it was among the inmates who had the fewest outside contacts that there was a strong negative relationship between integration and conformity. This indicates that it was those inmates who were in restrictive organizational climates and without ties to the outside world who most approximated the "solidary opposition" model of the inmate group. This finding demonstrates the impact of organizational policies on inmate adaptations. The inmates at Federal West who were most integrated, and lowest on outside contacts, were the most negative of all the subgroups examined. Not only did they have less contact with staff in general than the inmates at Federal East, but this group also had less contact with others outside the institution than their fellows at Federal West. Without prosocial ties within or without the institution they have indeed become prisonized. These data dramatically demonstrate the need for intensive staff-inmate interaction and the opportunity for inmates to maintain ties with families and friends outside the institution through letters, phone calls, visits, or furloughs. Without this it is more likely that these young men will be "banished again and again."

We found pluralistic ignorance to be extensive at both institutions, although it was more so at Federal West. Our prediction of a negative relationship between integration and pluralistic ignorance was not supported: those who were moderately integrated at Federal East were most accurate in predicting the responses of other inmates; at Federal West no consistent pattern appeared.

Interpersonal Relationships within the
Alternate Society

As has been found in numerous previous studies made in other settings, friendship choices of the inmates were closely related to physical proximity within the institution. To the extent that influence may follow friendship, it appears that the classification and separate housing of inmates in different units or institutions on the basis of criminal sophistication is a feasible and effective method of preventing or slowing the diffusion of criminal attitudes and techniques.

Friendship choices were found to be positively associated with the inmates' scores on our Similarity Index, which measures similarity between inmates simultaneously for nine variables. As predicted, this association between friendship and similarity was stronger at Federal West.

Of the individual personal characteristics affecting friendship choices, race was by far the most important. In the vast majority of instances the inmates named other inmates of the same race as their town trip choices. Especially noteworthy was the complete absence of friendship ties between blacks and Indians at Federal West; there were friendship ties between the white inmates and both of these minority groups. There was a slight tendency on the part of the older inmates to choose other older inmates as their town trip partners at both institutions. Only among the lower-class inmates at Federal West was there a noticeable within-class bias in the friendship choices.

Among the offense characteristics examined in relation to friendship choices, Type of Offense seemed to be the most related to the choices of the inmates. Public order offenders stood out as the group with the strongest self-preference ratio scores. While the other offense characteristics did not strongly influence friendship choices, there was a rather persistent tendency for the less serious offenders (i.e., those with fewer previous offenses, with public order offenses, with no previous institutionalization) to choose as town trip partners other inmates who were similar to themselves, especially at Federal West.

A similar patterning was found at both institutions for those inmates who had not received any major misconduct reports or who had never been in the segregation unit. Of the organizational characteristics examined, however, similarity in terms of length of stay was generally the most important.

In sum, we found in-group closure on a number of variables at the two institutions, although generally this closure was greater at Federal West. Since there were no institutional policies specifically designed to promote this type of closure, it can best be seen as a type of self-segregation. The extremely high self-preference ratios of the racial groups at Federal West were congruent with our on-site observations. The complete lack of friendship ties between blacks and Indians was congruent with reports from staff that a great deal of tension existed between these groups. These findings suggest the need for some form of "affirmative action" in institutions that house substantial numbers of ethnic minorities. Without such programs group animosities may develop that hinder both the rehabilitative efforts of the institution and the potential of the inmates to make a successful adjustment after release. These findings are also consistent with our previous argument that such problems will be exacerbated in a restrictive organizational climate. Friendship choices were also related to similarity of length of stay, a finding that was predicted and that is explainable in terms of similarity of interests and opportunities to establish friendships. Of greater significance, however, was the finding that inmates with less serious offense histories and with records of better institutional adjustment more often chose their friends from those inmates with similar characteristics. Since there were no official institutional policies designed to foster this, it represents a self-initiated effort on the part of a group of inmates to limit their associations within the institution. Would it not be desirable to facilitate such a process through organizational arrangements? Federal East utilized an elaborate classification system, which resulted in separate housing for the different types of inmates identified, but offense background was not a major factor in the classification procedure. Federal West utilized custody classifications, but these were used primarily to determine whether an inmate could be allowed to go outside the fenced perimeter of the institution; inmates of different custody classifications were more or less mixed randomly in the main housing units. Perhaps the more basic question that should be asked is whether young men who have committed few and relatively minor offenses should be institutionalized at all. If one were to look closely at the actual offenses that resulted in some of the inmates' being institutionalized, one would learn that some were there for stealing cookies from a store on an Indian reservation or for destroying interstate highway signs. It is questionable whether institutionalization that results in forced associations with more serious offenders is likely to be productive in the long run.

We had predicted that inmates would choose as friends other inmates who held conformity orientations similar to their own. This prediction was based on previous research, which had shown a strong relationship between attraction and congruity of attitudes, beliefs, and values. The data from Federal East supported our hypothesis; the data from Federal West did not. At both institutions the low conformity inmates showed the greatest degree of self-preference. One explanation offered for the lack of relationship between similarity of conformity orientations and friendship choices at Federal West was the greater amount of pluralistic ignorance that characterized the inmate group there. The more open atmosphere and the discussions among inmates and staff at Federal East made it more likely that the inmates knew where others stood on different issues; this same kind of openness did not appear to exist at Federal West, where the disparity between the privately held orientations and the perceived orientations of others was greater.

Leadership Patterns within the Alternate Society

Approximately one-fourth of the inmates at both institutions had been nominated as representation leaders; one-sixth of the inmates at both institutions were identified as being influential in the inmate group. There was considerable overlap between these two types of leadership groups, but they were far from being coterminous. We found that in some cases whether or not we found support for hypotheses depended on the leadership measure we used. Both representation and influence leadership were associated with length of stay and age at both institutions. There was a negative association at the two institutions between representation leadership and number of previous offenses, but a positive relationship between influence leadership and number of previous offenses. Similarly, we found a positive association between representation leadership and prosocial conformity orientations, but we found a negative association between influence leadership and prosocial conformity orientations. The inmates identified certain other inmates as being suited to deal with the administration, and while there was some overlap, they identified another group as being most influential among the inmates themselves. Certain inmates were seen as capable of fulfilling external liaison functions and others as performing certain internal control functions.

The identification of two leadership cadres is probably the most significant finding resulting from our examination of leadership patterns and has implications for both administrators and researchers. A fairly large number of institutions do utilize inmate councils as mechanisms for communication and participation in decisionmaking in prescribed areas. Our data indicated that such inmates may not be representative of the typical inmate or of influential leaders among the inmates; they may have been elected because they were seen as being acceptable to the administration. Elected inmate leaders should probably be viewed as communicators, rather than wielders of influence. This finding also has implications for researchers studying the inmate group. In some instances a positive association between leadership and another variable disappeared or became a negative association of equal strength when we interchanged our indicators of leadership status. If the inmates distinguish between two types of leaders, can researchers afford not to? Some of the apparent discrepancies in previous findings may be due to the different measures used to identify inmate leaders.

We had predicted that relatively cooperative and positive leaders would emerge in inmate groups found in permissive organizational climates and that just the opposite would be the case in restrictive organizational climates. As we noted above, whether or not there was an association between leadership and conformity orientations depended on the measure of leadership used. However, it should be pointed out that while the associations between leadership status and conformity orientations at Federal West paralleled that at Federal East, the associations at Federal West were of negligible strength. Thus it appears that certain relationships will vary from setting to setting. Given the patterns observed, we must conclude that there was no relationship between leadership status (measured by either of our operational measures) and conformity orientations at Federal West and that the relationship at Federal East was very much determined by the leadership measure we used. The inmates at Federal East did, however, report much more positive perceptions of their leaders than did the inmates at Federal West.

We had predicted that inmates would select as leaders other inmates who were similar to themselves in terms of certain personal, offense, and organizational characteristics and that the inmates at Federal West would do this more often than the inmates at Federal East. The distribution of Similarity Index scores of followers and leaders indicated that overall similarity was related to leadership choice at Federal West but not at Federal East.

Our examination of the relationship of leadership and similarity on individual characteristics produced mixed results, which defy simple summarization. Similarity in terms of race was clearly related to leadership choice at both institutions. While similarity was also related to the selection of leaders in several other instances, the self-preference ratios were not very large. Where they were large they were limited to only certain subgroups, e.g., only inmates who had been in the institution a long time tended to select as leaders other inmates who were similar to themselves. A number of the relationships examined reflected the findings reported above regarding the characteristics of the leaders. All categories of inmates at both Federal East and Federal West tended to overselect as leaders those inmates who were older, had no recorded previous offenses, and had committed a public order offense.

We also had predicted that inmates would select as leaders other inmates who had conformity orientations similar to their own. Briefly stated, this simply was not the case. The inmates selected other inmates whose orientations were similar to theirs about as often as we would expect on the basis of chance, but not much more often, if at all. We saw this as a result of the condition of pluralistic ignorance that prevailed at the two institutions and also as a result of some inmates' choosing as representation leaders inmates who would be acceptable to the staff rather than similar to themselves. Once again we are reminded not to assume that elected leaders actually "represent" the inmates who select them.

The Alternate Society: Synthesizing the Importation and Deprivation Models

We have, in the preceding pages, demonstrated quite clearly that the normative content and social structure of the alternate society of inmates vary from one organizational setting to another. In doing so we have also highlighted the importance of the deprivation model of prisonization. Yet, at the same time, it was shown that the importation model of prisonization is more useful for explaining the orientations of some inmates. These findings help us reconcile some of the differences in the previous literature. Certain earlier authors studying juveniles or young adult offenders have emphasized the importance of the organizational setting. Other authors studying older populations emphasized similarities across organizational settings and between organizational settings and the larger society in which they were located. We found that those inmates who were less involved in a life of crime (as measured by the number of previous offenses they were recorded as having committed) were affected significantly by the organizational climate in which they were located: those in a permissive organizational climate were much more likely to share staff-endorsed conformity orientations than were those in a restrictive organizational climate. Those inmates who were more involved in a life of crime (as indicated by an extensive record of previous offenses) were not affected by the organizational climate in which they were located: those in the permissive organizational climate were just as antisocially oriented as those in the restrictive organizational climate. It appears then that the deprivation model would be most appropriate in working with inexperienced offenders, while the importation model is of greater utility with more experienced offenders.

Looking Back, Looking Ahead

It is appropriate at this point to reflect on the strengths and weaknesses of this book and to make some suggestions for future research in this area.

A number of the strengths here are also weaknesses. This book involved a survey of propositions regarding the phenomenon of prisonization and friendship and leadership patterns in correctional institutions and the testing of these propositions against data gathered at two federal youth institutions. It was possible to test many of these propositions quite adequately, but others were impossible to test at all, since the data had been gathered as part of a larger study prior to the author's formulation of the research questions for this book. Some hypotheses had to be rewritten from their original form, and others had to be dropped completely simply because data were not available to test them.

In attempting to cover as broad an area as we have here, we have necessarily sacrificed depth for breadth. We have asked and answered many questions, although many not as thoroughly as we would have preferred. Our methodological approach has been a very basic one involving the examination of bivariate or trivariate relationships. Additional analyses utilizing multivariate techniques to ferret out the underlying dynamics and provide a more comprehensive picture of the relationships that exist among our variables is needed. For instance, in our analysis of those variables that were associated with leadership status and those variables for which similarity was related to friendship and leadership choices, we treated our predictor variables as independent of each other, when indeed some were correlated. Which of these variables provides the greatest predictive power? For which combination of variables may an interaction effect be present? These are important questions that we have not been able to address with the methodologies we have utilized.

A major strength of this book has been the utilization of more than one study site, making possible a comparative analysis. At the same time, however, it is necessary to remember that Federal East had been established relatively recently and, consequently may have been less typical than other similar but long-established institutions. Replication of these research questions in other institutional and noninstitutional settings would do much to advance our knowledge in this area.

One of our main purposes was to provide linkages to and to reconcile the apparently contradictory findings of previous studies. In this endeavor we have been at least moderately successful. We have painted a broad overview, have provided details reconciling previous studies, and have pointed to the need to qualify other findings and concepts. Hopefully we have added in some small way to the knowledge base on which future correctional researchers and administrators will build. At the same time we recognize the need to learn more of the details and the dynamics that underlie this broad picture if we are to understand the extent to which certain formal organizational arrangements facilitate or necessitate alternate informal social structures, which, in turn, may facilitate or impede the rehabilitation of offenders. Perhaps some day we may even be able to add a happy ending to a previously grim tale.

Bibliography

Adamek, Raymond J., and Dager, Edward Z. "Social Structure, Identification and Change in a Treatment-Oriented Institution." *American Sociological Review* 33 (1968): 932-943.

Akers, Ronald L.; Hayner, Norman S.; and Gruninger, Werner. "Homosexual and Drug Behavior in Prison: A Test of the Functional and Importation Models of the Inmate System." *Social Problems* 21 (1974): 410-422.

Atchley, Robert C., and McCabe, M. Patrick. "Socialization in Correctional Communities: A Replication." *American Sociological Review* 33 (1968): 774-785.

Berk, Bernard. "Informal Social Organization and Leadership among Inmates in Treatment and Custodial Prisons: A Comparative Study." Ph.D. dissertation, University of Michigan, 1961.

_____. "Organization Goals and Inmate Organization." In *Correctional Institutions*, edited by Robert Carter, Daniel Glaser, and Leslie T. Wilkins, pp. 233-247. Philadelphia: J.B. Lippincott Co., 1972.

Bescanceney, Paul H. "Impact of Therapeutic Goals on Client Organization." Mimeographed. Ann Arbor, Mich.: University of Michigan, 1960.

Blalock, Herbert M. *Social Statistics*. New York: McGraw-Hill Book Co., 1960.

Buffum, Peter C. *Homosexuality in Prisons*. Washington, D.C.: National Institute of Law Enforcement and Criminal Justice, 1972.

Bureau of Prisons. *Differential Treatment . . . a way to begin*. Washington, D.C.: U.S. Department of Justice, 1970.

Byrne, Donn. "Attitudes and Attraction." In *Advances in Experimental Social Psychology*, edited by Leonard Berkowitz, vol. 4, pp. 36-89. New York: Academic Press, 1969.

Clemmer, Donald. *The Prison Community*. 1940. Reissue. New York: Holt, Rinehart and Winston, 1958

Cline, Hugh F. "The Determinants of Normative Patterns in Correctional Institutions." In *Scandinavian Studies in Criminology*, edited by Nils Christie, vol. 2, pp. 173-184. Oslo: Oslo University Press, 1968.

Collins, Barry E., and Raven, Bertram H. "Group Structure: Attraction, Coalitions, Communication, and Power." In *The Handbook of Social Psychology*, edited by Garner Lindzey and Elliot Aronson, 2d ed., vol. 4, pp. 102-204. Reading, Mass.: Addison-Wesley Publishing Co., 1969.

Cressey, Donald R., ed. *The Prison; Studies in Institutional Organization and Change*. New York: Holt, Rinehart and Winston, 1966.

Criswell, Joan H. "Foundations of Sociometric Measurement." *Sociometry* 9 (1946): 7-13.

_____ . "The Measurement of Group Integration." *Sociometry* 10 (1947): 259-267.

_____ . "Notes on the Constant Frame of Reference Problem." *Sociometry* 10 (1950): 93-107.

_____ . "Sociometric Measurement and Chance." *Sociometry* 7 (1944): 415-421.

_____ . "Sociometric Methods of Measuring Group Preferences." *Sociometry* 6 (1943): 398-408.

_____ . "A Sociometric Study of Race Cleavage in the Classroom." *Archives of Psychology* 33, No. 235 (1939): 1-82.

Davies, Vernon. "The Measurement of Disproportionality." *Sociometry* 23 (1960): 407-414.

Dickson, Donald T. "Environments, Goals and Technology: An Analysis of Organizational Change in a New Juvenile Correctional Institution." Ph.D. dissertation, University of Michigan, 1973.

Eaton, Joseph. *Stone Walls Do Not A Prison Make*. Springfield, Ill.: Charles Thomas, 1962.

Empey, LaMar T. "Conformity and Deviance in the Situation of Company." *American Sociological Review* 33 (1968): 760-774.

_____ and Lubeck, Steven G. *Explaining Delinquency*. Lexington, Mass.: Lexington Books, 1971.

_____ and Rabow, Jerome. "The Provo Experiment in Delinquency Rehabilitation." *American Sociological Review* 26 (1961): 679-696.

Erickson, Maynard L., and Empey, LaMar T. "Court Records, Undetected Delinquency and Decision Making." *Journal of Criminal Law, Criminology and Police Science* 54 (1963): 456-469.

Festinger, Leon. "A Theory of Social Comparison Processes." *Human Relations* 7 (1954): 117-140.

_____ . *A Theory of Cognitive Dissonance*. Stanford: Stanford University Press, 1957.

Fisher, Sethard. "Informal Organization in a Correctional Setting." *Social Problems* 13 (1965): 214-222.

Gagnon, John H., and Simon, William. "The Social Meaning of Prison Homosexuality." In *Correctional Institutions*, edited by Robert Carter, Daniel Glaser, and Leslie T. Wilkins, pp. 221-232. Philadelphia: J.B. Lippincott, 1972.

Galtung, Johan. "Prison: The Organization of Dilemma." In *The Prison: Studies in Institutional Organizational and Change*, edited by Donald R. Cressey, pp. 107-145. New York: Holt, Rinehart and Winston, 1961.

Garabedian, Peter G. "Social Roles and Processes of Socialization in the Prison Community." *Social Problems* 11 (1963): 139-152.

_____ . "Western Penitentiary: A Study in Social Organization." Unpublished Ph.D. dissertation, University of Washington, 1959.

Garrity, Donald L. "The Prison as a Rehabilitation Agency." In *The Prison: Studies in Institutional Organization and Change*, edited by Donald R. Cressey, pp. 358-380. New York: Holt, Rinehart and Winston, 1961.

Giallombardo, Rose. *Society of Women: A Study of a Women's Prison*. New York: John Wiley and Sons, 1966.

_____ . *The Social World of Imprisoned Girls*. New York: John Wiley and Sons, 1974.

_____ . "Social Roles in a Prison for Women." *Social Problems* 13 (1966): 268-288.

Gibb, Cecil A. "Leadership." In *The Handbook of Social Psychology*, edited by Gardner Lindzey and Elliot Aronson, 2d edition, vol. 4, pp. 205-282. Reading, Mass.: Addison-Wesley Publishing Co., 1969.

Glaser, Daniel. *The Effectiveness of a Prison and Parole System*. Indianapolis: Bobbs-Merrill Co., 1964.

Goffman, Irving. "On the Characteristics of Total Institutions: Staff-Inmate Relations." In *The Prison: Studies in Institutional Organization and Change*, edited by Donald R. Cressey, pp. 68-106. New York: Holt, Rinehart and Winston, 1961.

Gold, Martin. *Delinquent Behavior in an American City*. Monterey, Calif.: Brooks Cole Publishing Co., 1970.

Gross, Edward. "Universities as Organizations: A Research Approach." *American Sociological Review* 33 (1968): 518-544.

Grosser, George P. "The Role of Informal Inmate Groups in Change of Values." *Children* 5 (1958): 25-29.

Grusky, Oscar. "Organizational Goals and the Behavior of Informal Leaders." *American Journal of Sociology* 65 (1959): 59-67.

_____ . "Treatment Goals and Organizational Behavior: A Study of an Experimental Prison Camp." Ph.D. dissertation, University of Michigan, 1957.

Hall, John W. "A Comparison of Halpin and Craft's Organizational Climates and Likert's Organizational Systems." *Administrative Science Quarterly* 17 (1972): 586-590.

Hare, A. Paul. *Handbook of Small Group Research*. New York: The Free Press, 1962.

Hazelrigg, Lawrence, editor. *Prison within Society*. Garden City, New York: Anchor Books, 1969.

Heider, Fritz. *The Psychology of Interpersonal Relations*. New York: John Wiley and Sons, 1958.

Hulin, C.L. and Maker, B.A. "Changes in Attitudes toward Law Concomitant with Imprisonment." *Journal of Criminal Law and Criminology* 50 (1959): 245-248.

Irwin, John. *The Felon*. Englewood Cliffs, N.J.: Prentice-Hall, 1970.

———. "The Prison Experience: The Convict World." In *Correctional Institutions*, edited by Robert Carter, Daniel Glaser, and Leslie T. Wilkins, pp. 173-192. Philadelphia: J.B. Lippincott Co., 1972.

——— and Cressey, Donald. "Thieves, Convicts and the Inmate Culture." *Social Problems* 10 (1962): 142-155.

Jennings, Helen Hall. *Leadership and Isolation; A Study of Personality in Inter-Personal Relations*. New York: Longmans, Green, and Co., 1950.

Jensen, Gary F., and Jones, Dorothy. "Perspectives on Inmate Culture: A Study of Women in Prison." *Social Forces* 54 (1976): 590-602.

Johnson, Elmer. "Sociology of Confinement: Assimilation and the Prison 'Rat.' " In *Correctional Institutions*, edited by Robert Carter, Daniel Glaser, and Leslie T. Wilkins, pp. 193-202. Philadelphia: J.B. Lippincott Co., 1972.

Jones, James A. " The Nature of Compliance in Correctional Institutions for Juvenile Offenders." *Journal of Research in Crime and Delinquency* 1 (1964): 83-95.

Kassebaum, Gene; Ward, David; and Wilner, Daniel. *Prison Treatment and Parole Survival: An Empirical Assessment*. New York: John Wiley and Sons, 1971.

King, Morton B. Jr. "Sociometric Status and Sociometric Choice." *Social Forces* 39 (1961): 199-206.

Lerman, Paul. "Individual Values, Peer Values, and Subculture Delinquency." *American Sociological Review* 33 (1968): 219-235.

Lindzey, Gardner, and Byrne, Donn. "Measurement of Social Choice and Interpersonal Attractiveness." In *The Handbook of Social Psychology*, edited by Gardner Lindzey and Elliot Aronson, 2d ed., vol. 2, pp. 452-525. Reading, Mass.: Addison-Wesley Publishing Co., 1968.

Loomis, Charles P. "Ethnic Cleavages in the Southwest as Reflected in Two High Schools." *Sociometry* 6 (1943): 7-26.

——— and Pepinsky, H.B. "Sociometry, 1937-1947: Theory and Methods." *Sociometry* 11 (1948): 262-286.

McCleary, Richard H. "Authoritarianism and the Belief System of Incorrigibles." In *The Prison: Studies in Institutional Organization and Change*, edited by Donald R. Cressey, pp. 260-306. New York: Holt, Rinehart and Winston, 1961.

———. "The Governmental Process and Informal Social Control." In *The Prison: Studies in Institutional Organization and Change*, edited by Donald R. Cressey, pp. 149-188. New York: Holt, Rinehart and Winston, 1961.

McCorkle, Lloyd W. and Korn, Richard. "Resocialization within the Walls." *The Annals* 293 (1954): 88-98.

McDill, Edward L.; Rigsby, Leo C.; and Meyers, Edmund D. Jr. "Educational Climates of High Schools: Their Effects and Sources." *American Journal of Sociology* 74 (1969): 567-586.

Mathieson, Thomas. "Sociology of Prisons: Problems for Future Research." *British Journal of Sociology* 17 (1966): 360-379.

_____ . "Functional Equivalent to Inmate Cohesion." *Human Organization* 27 (1968): 117-124.

_____ . *Across the Boundaries of Organizations.* Berkeley: Glendessary Press, 1971.

Moreno, J.L. et al. editors. *The Sociometry Reader.* Glencoe, Ill.: The Free Press, 1960.

_____ and Jennings, Helen Hall. "Statistics of Social Configurations." *Sociometry* 1 (1938): 342-374.

Morrison, Denton E. and Hershel, Ramon E. *The Significance Test Controversy—A Reader.* Chicago: Aldine Publishing Co., 1970.

Mueller, John H.; Schuessler, Karl F.; and Costner, Herbert L. *Statistical Reasoning in Sociology.* 2d ed. Boston: Houghton Mifflin Co., 1970.

Newcomb, Theodore M. *The Acquaintance Process.* New York: Holt, Rinehart and Winston, 1961.

Ohlin, Lloyd E., and Lawrence, William C. "Social Interaction among Clients as a Treatment Problem." *Social Work* 4 (1959): 3-14.

Payne, Roy L., and Mansfield. "Relationships of Perceptions of Organizational Climate to Organizational Structure, Context and Hierarchical Position." *Administrative Science Quarterly* 18 (1973): 515-526.

Pepitone, Albert. *Attraction and Hostility.* New York: Atherton, 1964.

Perrow, Charles. "The Analysis of Goals in Complex Organizations." *American Sociological Review* 26 (1961): 854-866.

Polsky, Howard W. "Changing Delinquent Subcultures: A Social Psychological Approach." *Social Work* 4 (1959): 3-16.

_____ . *Cottage Six.* New York: John Wiley and Sons, 1965.

Priest, Robert F., and Sawyer, Jack. "Proximity and Peership: Bases of Balance in Interpersonal Attraction." *American Journal of Sociology* 72 (1967): 633-649.

Roebuck, Julian. "A Critique of 'Thieves, Convicts and the Inmate Culture.' " *Social Problems* 11 (1963): 193-200.

Sarri, Rosemary C. "Organizational Patterns and Client Perspectives in Juvenile Correctional Institutions: A Comparative Study." Ph.D. dissertation, University of Michigan, 1962.

Schrag, Clarence. "Leadership among Prison Inmates." *American Sociological Review* 19 (1954): 37-42.

_____ . "Some Foundations for a Theory of Correction." In *Correctional Institutions*, edited by Robert Carter, Daniel Glaser, and Leslie T. Wilkins, pp. 149-172. Philadelphia: J.B. Lippincott Co., 1972.

Schwartz, Barry. "Pre-Institutional vs. Situational Influence in a Correctional Community." *The Journal of Criminal Law, Criminology and Police Science* 62 (1971): 532-542.

Secord, P.F., and Backman, C.W. "Interpersonal Congruency, Perceived Similarity and Friendship." *Sociometry* 27 (1964): 115-127.

Seeman, Melvin. "Alienation and Social Learning in a Reformatory." *American Sociological Review* 69 (1963): 270-284.

Sherif, M. *An Outline of Social Psychology.* New York: Harper, 1948.

Shils, Edward A. "Primary Groups in the American Army." In *Continuities in Social Research: Studies in the Scope and Method of the "American Soldier,"* edited by Robert K. Merton and Paul F. Lazarsfeld, pp. 19-22. Glencoe, Ill.: The Free Press, 1950.

Short, James F., Jr., and Strodtbeck, Fred L. *Group Process and Gang Delinquency.* Chicago: University of Chicago Press, 1965.

Siegel, Sidney. *Nonparametric Statistics.* New York: McGraw-Hill Book Co., 1956.

Simpson, J.E. et al. "Institutionalization as Perceived by the Juvenile Offender." *Sociology and Social Research* 48 (1963): 13-23.

Stogdill, Ralph M. *Handbook of Leadership; A Survey of Theory and Research.* New York: The Free Press, 1974.

Street, David. "Inmate Social Organization: A Comparative Study of Juvenile Correctional Institutions." Ph.D. dissertation, University of Michigan, 1962.

_____ . "The Inmate Group in Custodial and Treatment Settings." In *Prison within Society*, edited by Lawrence Hazelrigg, pp. 199-228. Garden City, N.Y.: Anchor Books, 1969.

_____ ; Vinter, Robert; and Perrow, Charles. *Organization for Treatment.* New York: The Free Press, 1966.

Sykes, Gresham M. *The Society of Captives; A Study of a Maximum Security Prison.* New York: Atheneum, 1966.

_____ . "The Corruption of Authority and Rehabilitation." *Social Forces* 34 (1956): 275-262.

_____ . "Men, Merchants and Toughs: A Study of Reactions to Imprisonment." *Social Problems* 4 (1956): 130-138.

_____ and Messinger, Sheldon L. "The Inmate Social System." In *Theoretical Studies in Social Organization of the Prison*, Social Science Research Council, pamphlet 15, pp. 5-19. New York, 1960.

Thomas, Charles W. "Toward a More Inclusive Model of the Inmate Contraculture." *Criminology* 8 (1970): 251-262.

_____ and Foster, Samuel C. "Prisonization in the Inmate Contraculture." *Social Problems* 20 (1972): 229-239.

Thompson, James D., and McEwen, William J. "Organizational Goals and Environment: Goal Setting as an Interactive Process." *American Sociological Review* 23 (1958): 23-31.

Tittle, Charles R. "Inmate Organization: Sex Differentiation and the Influence of Criminal Subcultures." *American Sociological Review* 34
(1969):492-504.

_____ and Tittle D.P. "Social Organization of Prisoners: An Empirical
Test." *Social Forces* 43 (1964): 216-221.

Trasler, Gordon. "The Social Relations of Persistent Offenders." In *Correctional Institutions*, edited by Robert Carter, Daniel Glaser, and
Leslie T. Wilkins, pp. 203-212. Philadelphia: J.B. Lippincott Co., 1972.

Vinter, Robert, and Janowitz, Morris. "Effective Institutions for Juvenile
Offenders: A Research Statement." *Social Service Review* 33 (1959):
118-131.

_____ and Perrow, Charles. "Client Organization in the Correctional Institution." Mimeographed. Ann Arbor, Mich.: University of Michigan,
1960.

_____ and Sarri, Rosemary C. *Federal Correctional Program for Young
Offenders: A Comparative Study.* Washington, D.C.: U.S. Department
of Justice, 1974.

Voss, Harland. "Differential Association and Containment Theory."
Social Forces 47 (1969): 381-391.

Vreeland, Francis McLennan. "Social Relationships in the College Frater-
nity." *Sociometry* 5 (1942): 151-162.

Watt, N., and Maher, B.A. "Prisoners' Attitudes towards Home and the
Judicial System." *Journal of Criminal Law and Criminology* 49 (1958):
327-330.

Weber, Louis C. "A Study of Peer Acceptance among Delinquent Girls."
Sociometry 13 (1950): 363-381.

Weinberg, S. Kirson. "Aspects of the Prison's Social Structure." *American
Journal of Sociology* 47 (1942): 717-726.

Wellford, Charles. "Factors Associated with Adoption of the Inmate Code:
A Study of Normative Socialization." *Journal of Criminal Law,
Criminology and Police Science* 58 (1969): 197-203.

Wheeler, Stanton. "Social Organization in a Correctional Community."
Ph.D. dissertation, University of Washington, 1958.

_____ . "Role Conflict in Correctional Communities." In *The Prison:
Studies in Institutional Organization and Change,* edited by Donald R.
Cressey, pp. 229-259. New York: Holt, Rinehart and Winston, 1961.

_____ . "Socialization in Correctional Communities." *American
Sociological Review* 26 (1961): 697-712.

_____ , editor. *Controlling Delinquents.* New York: John Wiley and Sons,
1968.

Williams, Jay R., and Gold, Martin. "From Delinquent Behavior to Official Delinquency." *Social Problems* 20 (1972): 209-229.

Wilson, Thomas P. "Patterns of Management and Adaptations to Organizational Roles: A Study of Prison Inmates." In *Correctional Institutions,* edited by Robert Carter, Daniel Glaser, and Leslie T. Wilkins; pp. 248-262. Philadelphia: J.B. Lippincott Co., 1972.

Zald, Mayer. "The Correctional Institution for Juvenile Offenders: An Analysis of Organization Character." *Social Problems* 8 (1960):57-67.

_____ . "Multiple Goals and Staff Structure: A Comparative Study of Correctional Institutions for Juvenile Delinquents." Ph.D. dissertation, University of Michigan, 1960.

Index

About the Author

John A. Slosar, Jr., received the Master of Social Work and the Ph.D. in Social Work and Sociology from the University of Michigan. He is an associate professor of social work in the School of Social Service at Saint Louis University. He was previously a research associate with the School of Social Work at The University of Michigan. His previous publications include participant observation research on urban life and the counterproductive effects of social intervention. He is currently involved in the evaluation of juvenile corrections.

UNIVERSITY